Allyn and Bacon

Quick Guide to the Internet
for
Speech Communication

2000 Edition

Terrence A. Doyle, Ph. D.
Northern Virginia Community College

Doug Gotthoffer
California State University–Northridge

Allyn and Bacon
Boston • London • Toronto • Sydney • Tokyo • Singapore

Vice President and Director, Allyn and Bacon Interactive: Kevin B. Stone
Multimedia Editor: Marnie S. Greenhut
Editorial Production Administrator, Media: Robert Tonner
Cover Designer: Jennifer Hart
Editorial Production Service: Omegatype Typography, Inc.

NOTICE: Between the time web site information is gathered and then published it is not unusual for some sites to have closed. Also, the transcription of URLs can result in unintended typographical errors. The publisher would appreciate notification where these occcur so that they may be corrected in subsequent editions. Thank you.

TRADEMARK CREDITS: Where information was available, trademarks and registered trademarks are indicated below. When detailed information was not available, the publisher has indicated trademark status with an initial capital where those names appear in the text.

Macintosh is a registered trademark of Apple Computer, Inc.

Microsoft is a registered trademark of Microsoft Corporation. Windows, Windows95, and Microsoft Internet Explorer are trademarks of Microsoft Corporation.

Netscape and the Netscape Navigator logo are registered trademarks of Netscape Communications Corporation.

ISBN 0-205-30969-0

Printed in the United States of America

10 9 8 7 6 5 4   02 01 00 99

Contents

Part 1   Introduction to the Internet

Some Things You Ought to Know   1
A Brief History of the Internet   3
Using the World Wide Web for Research   4
In the Name of the Page   6
The URL Exposed   7
Getting There from Here   9
You Can Go Home (and to Other Pages) Again   11
Searching and Search Engines   11
Internet Gold Is Where You Find It   12
The (E)mail Goes Through   18
Welcome to the Internet, Miss Manners   21
Keeping Things to Yourself   22
A Discussion of Lists   24
And Now the News(group)   27
Welcome to the Internet, Miss Manners—Again   29
Give Your Web Browser Some Personality—Yours   31
Speech Communication on the Internet   32
Using the Internet to Relate   32
Multimedia and the Internet   41
Setting Up Your Own Home Page on the Web   41
Critical Evaluation   47

Part 2   Speech Communication Online Activities

Strategy I: Finding a Speech Topic   51
Exercise: 5W's and How for Informative Speeches   54
Strategy II: Finding and Evaluating Evidence   57
Exercise: Finding and Evaluating Sources of Information
     on the Web   59
Exercise: Persuasive Speaking on Legislative Topics   63
Exercise: Do You Agree with the ACLU?   67
Strategy III: Using Reference Sources: Encyclopedias, Dictionaries,
     Glossaries, and Thesauri   69
Exercise: Look It Up   69
Strategy IV: Analyzing Your Audience   72
Exercise: Draw a Demographic and Psychographic Profile   73

SPEECH COMMUNICATION RELATED WEBSITES   78
General Search Engines   78
Topical Browsers   80
Other Searching Tools   82
Advocacy Groups   93
Encyclopedias and Reference Sources   96
Writing Tools   100
Newspapers   102
Wire Services   104
Online Magazines   105
Broadcast News Networks   109
Legislative   110
Judicial   113
Sources for Audience Analysis   116
Multimedia   119
Live Chat   122
Live Events   123
Historical Archives   124

DOCUMENTATION   127
Your Citation for Exemplary Research   127
    MLA Style   128
    APA Style   130

Glossary   135

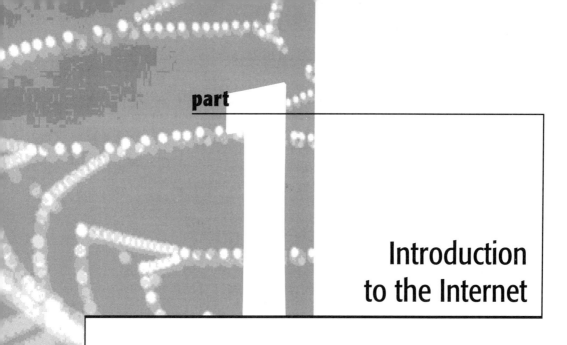

Introduction to the Internet

You're about to embark on an exciting experience as you become one of the millions of citizens of the Internet. In spite of what you might have heard, the Internet can be mastered by ordinary people before they earn a college degree and even if they're not majoring in rocket science.

Some Things You Ought to Know

Much of the confusion over the Internet comes from two sources. One is terminology. Just as the career you're preparing for has its own special vocabulary, so does the Internet. You'd be hard pressed to join in the shoptalk of archeologists, librarians, or carpenters if you didn't speak their language. Don't expect to plop yourself down in the middle of the Internet without some buzzwords under your belt, either.

The second source of confusion is that there are often many ways to accomplish the same ends on the Internet. This is a direct by-product of the freedom so highly cherished by Net citizens. When someone has an idea for doing something, he or she puts it out there and lets the Internet community decide its merits. As a result, it's difficult to put down in writing the *one exact* way to send email or find information on slugs or whatever.

In addition, there are differences in the workings of a PC or Mac and the various versions of the two major browsers, Netscape Communicator (or Navigator) and Internet Explorer. If you can't find a particular command or function mentioned in the book on your computer, chances are it's there, but in a different place or with a slightly different name. Check the manual or online help that came with your computer, or ask a more computer-savvy friend or professor.

And relax. Getting up to speed on the Internet takes a little time, but the effort will be well rewarded. Approach learning your way around the Internet with the same enthusiasm and curiosity you approach learning your way around a new college campus. This isn't a competition. Nobody's keeping score. And the only winner will be you.

In *Understanding Media,* Marshall McLuhan presaged the existence of the Internet when he described electronic media as an extension of our central nervous system. On the other hand, today's students introduced to the Internet for the first time describe it as "Way cool."

No matter which description you favor, you are immersed in a period in our culture that is transforming the way we live by transforming the nature of the information we live by. As recently as 1980, intelligence was marked by "knowing things." If you were born in that year, by the time you were old enough to cross the street by yourself, that definition had changed radically. Today, in a revolution that makes McLuhan's vision tangible, events, facts, rumors, and gossip are distributed instantly to all parts of the global body. The effects are equivalent to a shot of electronic adrenaline. No longer the domain of the privileged few, information is shared by all the inhabitants of McLuhan's global village. Meanwhile, the concept of information as intelligence feels as archaic as a television remote control with a wire on it (ask your parents about that).

With hardly more effort than it takes to rub your eyes open in the morning you can connect with the latest news, with gossip about your favorite music group or TV star, with the best places to eat on spring break, with the weather back home, or with the trials and tribulations of that soap opera character whose life conflicts with your history class.

You can not only carry on a real-time conversation with your best friend at a college half a continent away you can see and hear her, too. Or, you can play interactive games with a dozen or more world-wide, world-class, challengers; and that's just for fun.

When it comes to your education, the Internet has shifted the focus from amassing information to putting that information to use. Newspaper and magazine archives are now almost instantly available, as are the contents of many reference books. Distant and seemingly unapproachable, experts are found answering questions in discussion groups or in electronic newsletters.

The Internet also addresses the major problem facing all of us in our split-second, efficiency-rated culture: Where do we find the time? The

Internet allows professors and students to keep in touch, to collaborate and learn, without placing unreasonable demands on individual schedules. Professors are posting everything from course syllabi to homework solutions on the Internet, and are increasingly answering questions online, all in an effort to ease the pressure for face-to-face meetings by supplementing them with cyberspace offices. The Internet enables students and professors to expand office hours into a twenty-four-hour-a-day, seven-day-a-week operation. Many classes have individual sites at which enrolled students can gather electronically to swap theories, ideas, resources, gripes, and triumphs.

By freeing us from some of the more mundane operations of information gathering, and by sharpening our information-gathering skills in other areas, the Internet encourages us to be more creative and imaginative. Instead of devoting most of our time to gathering information and precious little to analyzing and synthesizing it, the Internet tips the balance in favor of the skills that separate us from silicon chips. Other Internet citizens can gain the same advantage, however, and as much as the Internet ties us together, it simultaneously emphasizes our individual skills—our ability to connect information in new, meaningful, and exciting ways. Rarely have we had the opportunity to make connections and observations on such a wide range of topics, to create more individual belief systems, and to chart a path through learning that makes information personally useful and meaningful.

part

1

A Brief History of the Internet

The 20th century's greatest advance in personal communication and freedom of expression began as a tool for national defense. In the mid-1960s, the Department of Defense was searching for an information analogy to the new Interstate Highway System, a way to move computations and computing resources around the country in the event the Cold War caught fire. The immediate predicament, however, had to do with the Defense Department's budget, and the millions of dollars spent on computer research at universities and think tanks. Much of these millions was spent on acquiring, building, or modifying large computer systems to meet the demands of the emerging fields of computer graphics, artificial intelligence, and multiprocessing (where one computer was shared among dozens of different tasks).

While this research was distributed across the country, the unwieldy, often temperamental, computers were not. Though researchers at MIT had spare time on their computer, short of packing up their notes and traveling to Massachusetts, researchers at Berkeley had no way to use it. Instead, Berkeley computer scientists would wind up duplicating MIT hardware in California. Wary of being accused of re-inventing the wheel, the Advanced Research Projects Agency (ARPA), the funding arm of the Defense Department, invested in the ARPANET, a private network that would allow disparate computer systems to communicate with each other. Researchers could remain ensconced among their colleagues at their home campuses while using computing resources at government research sites thousands of miles away.

A small cadre of ARPANET citizens soon began writing computer programs to perform little tasks across the Internet. Most of these programs, while ostensibly meeting immediate research needs, were written for the challenge of writing them. These programmers, for example, created the first email systems. They also created games like Space Wars and Adventure. Driven in large part by the novelty and practicality of email, businesses and institutions accepting government research funds begged and borrowed their way onto the ARPANET, and the number of connections swelled.

part
1

As the innocence of the 1960s gave way the business sense of the 1980s, the government eased out of the networking business, turning the ARPANET (now Internet) over to its users. While we capitalize the word "Internet", it may surprise you to learn there is no "Internet, Inc.," no business in charge of this uniquely postmodern creation. Administration of this world-wide communication complex is still handled by the cooperating institutions and regional networks that comprise the Internet. The word "Internet" denotes a specific interconnected network of networks, and not a corporate entity.

Using the World Wide Web for Research

Just as no one owns the worldwide communication complex that is the Internet, there is no formal organization among the collection of hundreds of thousands of computers that make up the part of the Net called the World Wide Web.

If you've never seriously used the Web, you are about to take your first steps on what can only be described as an incredible journey. Initially, though, you might find it convenient to think of the Web as a giant television network with millions of channels. It's safe to say that, among all these channels, there's something for you to watch. Only, how to find it? You could click through the channels one by one, of course, but by the time you found something of interest it would (1) be over or (2) leave you wondering if there wasn't something better on that you're missing.

A more efficient way to search for what you want would be to consult some sort of TV listing. While you could skim through pages more rapidly than channels, the task would still be daunting. A more creative approach would allow you to press a button on your remote control that would connect you to a channel of interest; what's more, that channel would contain the names (or numbers) of other channels with similar programs. Those channels in turn would contain information about other channels. Now you could zip through this million-channel universe, touching down only at programs of potential interest. This seems far more effective than the hunt-and-peck method of the traditional couch potato.

If you have a feel for how this might work for television, you have a feel for what it's like to journey around (or surf) the Web. Instead of channels on the Web, we have *Web sites*. Each site contains one or more *pages*. Each page may contain, among other things, links to other pages, either in the same site or in other sites, anywhere in the world. These other pages may elaborate on the information you're looking at or may direct you to related but not identical information, or even provide contrasting or contradictory points of view; and, of course, these pages could have links of their own.

Web sites are maintained by businesses, institutions, affinity groups, professional organizations, government departments, and ordinary people anxious to express opinions, share information, sell products, or provide services. Because these Web sites are stored electronically, updating them is more convenient and practical than updating printed media. That makes Web sites far more dynamic than other types of research material you may be used to, and it means a visit to a Web site can open up new opportunities that weren't available as recently as a few hours ago.

Hypertext and Links

The invention that unveils these revolutionary possibilities is called *hypertext*. Hypertext is a technology for combining text, graphics, sounds, video, and links on a single World Wide Web page. Click on a link and you're transported, like Alice falling down the rabbit hole, to a new page, a new address, a new environment for research and communication.

Links come in three flavors: text, picture, and hot spot. A text link may be a letter, a word, a phrase, a sentence, or any contiguous combination of text characters. You can identify text links at a glance because

Text Link

Picture Link

Text links are underlined and set of in color. Picture links are set off by a colored border. Hot spots carry no visual identification.

the characters are <u>underlined</u>, and are often displayed in a unique color, setting the link apart from the rest of the text on the page. Picture links are pictures or other graphic elements. On the Web, a picture may not only be worth a thousand words, but it may also be the start of a journey into a whole new corner of cyberspace.

The third kind of link, the hot spot, is neither underlined nor bordered, a combination which would make it impossible to spot, were it not for a Web convention that offers you a helping hand finding all types of links. This helping hand is, well, a hand. Whenever the mouse cursor passes over a link, the cursor changes from an arrow to a hand. Wherever you see the hand icon, you can click and retrieve another Web page. Sweep the cursor over an area of interest, see the hand, follow the link, and you're surfing the Web.

In the Name of the Page

Zipping around the Web in this way may seem exciting, even serendipitous, but it's also fraught with perils. How, for instance, do you revisit a page of particular interest? Or share a page with a classmate? Or cite a page as a reference for a professor? Web page designers assign names, or titles, to their pages; unfortunately, there's nothing to prevent two designers from assigning the same title to different pages.

An instrument that uniquely identifies Web pages does exist. It's called a Universal Resource Locator (URL), the cyber-signposts of the World Wide Web. URLs contain all the information necessary to locate:

- the page containing the information you're looking for;
- the computer that hosts (stores) that page of information;
- the form the information is stored in.

A typical URL looks like this:

```
http://www.abacon.com/index.html
```

You enter it into the **Location** or **Address** field at the top of your browser window. Hit the **Return** (or **Enter**) key and your browser will deliver to your screen the exact page specified. When you click on a link, you're actually using a shorthand alternative to typing the URL yourself because the browser does it for you. In fact, if you watch the "Location" or "Address" field when you click on a link, you'll see its contents change to the URL you're traveling to.

part

1

The URL Exposed

How does your browser—or the whole World Wide Web structure, for that matter—know where you're going? As arcane as the URL appears, there is a logical explanation to its apparent madness. (This is true not only of URLs but also of your computer experience in general. Because a computer's "intelligence" only extends to following simple instructions exactly, most of the commands, instructions, and procedures you'll encounter have simple underlying patterns. Once you familiarize yourself with these patterns, you'll find you're able to make major leaps in your understanding of new Internet features.)

To unscramble the mysteries of World Wide Web addresses, we'll start at the end of the URL and work our way toward the front.

```
/index.html
```

This is the name of a single file or document. Eventually, the contents of this file/document will be transferred over the Internet to your computer.

However, because there are undoubtedly thousands of files on the Internet with this name, we need to clarify our intentions a bit more.

```
www.abacon.com
```

This is the name of a particular Internet *Web server*, a computer whose job it is to forward Web pages to you on request. By Internet convention, this name is unique. The combination of

```
www.abacon.com/index.html
```

identifies a unique file/document on a unique Web server on the World Wide Web. No other file has this combined address, so there's no question about which file/document to transfer to you.

The characters *http://* at the beginning of the URL identify the method by which the file/document will be transferred. The letters stand for **HyperText Transfer Protocol**.

part

1

Quick Check

Don't Be Lost In (Hyper)Space

Let's pause for a quick check of your Web navigation skills. Look at the sample web page on the next page. How many links does it contain?

Did you find all five? That's right, five:

- The word "links" in the second line below the seaside picture;
- The sentence "What about me?";
- The word "cyberspace" in the quick brown fox sentence;
- The red and white graphic in the lower left-hand corner of the page. The blue border around it matches the blue of the text links;
- The hot spot in the seaside picture. We know there's at least one link in the picture, because the cursor appears as a hand. (There may be more hot spots on the page, but we can't tell from this picture alone.)

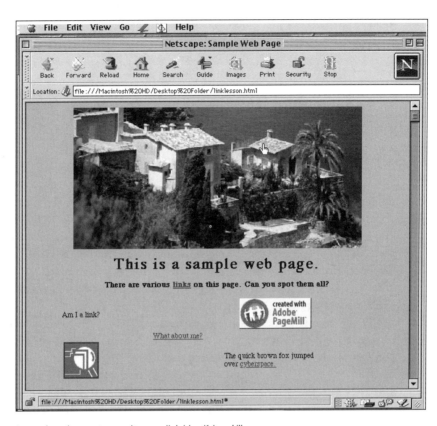

A sample web page to exercise your link identifying skills.

Getting There from Here

Now you know that a URL uniquely identifies a page and that links used as shorthand for URLs enable you to travel from page to page in the Web; but what if a link takes you someplace you don't want to go? Missing page messages take several forms, such as URL 404, Object not on this server, Missing Object, Page not Found, but they all lead to the same place—a dead end. The page specified by the link or URL no longer exists. There are many reasons for missing pages. You may have entered the URL incorrectly. Every character must be precise and no spaces are allowed. More than likely, though, especially if you arrived here via a link, the page you're after has been moved or removed. Remember, anybody can create a link to any page. In the spirit of the Internet, there are no forms to fill out, no procedures to follow. That's the good news. The bad news is that the owner of a page is under no

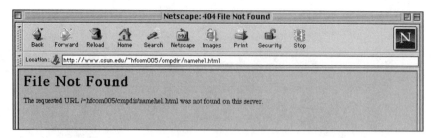

A missing page message, an all too common road hazard on the information superhighway.

obligation to inform the owners of links pointing to it that the page lo-cation has changed. In fact, there's no way for the page owner to even know about all the links to her page. Yes, the Internet's spirit of inde-pendence proves frustrating sometimes, but you'll find these small incon-veniences are a cheap price to pay for the benefits you receive. Philosophy aside, though, we're still stuck on a page of no interest to us. The best strategy is to back up and try another approach.

part
1

Every time you click on the **Back** button, you return to the previous page you visited. That's because your browser keeps track of the pages you visit and the order in which you visit them. The **Back** icon, and its counterpart, the **Forward** icon, allow you to retrace the steps, forward and backward, of your cyberpath. Sometimes you may want to move two, three, or a dozen pages at once. Although you can click the **Back** or **Forward** icons multiple times, Web browsers offer an easier navigation shortcut. If you use Netscape, clicking on the **Go** menu in the menu bar displays a list of your most recently visited pages, in the order you've been there. Unlike the **Back** or **Forward** icons, you can select any page from the menu, and a single click takes you directly there. There's no need to laboriously move one page a time. If you use Internet Explorer, you can click on the **History** button in the Explorer bar to see a list of links you visited in previous days and weeks, or press the arrow at the end of the Address bar to see previously visited links.

Quick Check

As a quick review, here's what we know about navigating the Web so far:

- Enter a URL directly into the Location field;
- Click on a link;
- Use the **Back** or **Forward** icons;
- Select a page from the **Go** menu.

You Can Go Home (and to Other Pages) Again

How do we return to a page hours, days, or even months later? One way is to write down the URLs of every page we may want to revisit. There's got to be a better way, and there is: We call them bookmarks (on Netscape Communicator) or favorites (on Microsoft Internet Explorer).

Like their print book namesakes, Web bookmarks (and favorites) flag specific Web pages. Selecting an item from the **Bookmark/Favorites** menu, like selecting an item from the **Go** menu, is the equivalent of entering a URL into the **Location** field of your browser, except that items in the **Bookmark/Favorites** menu are ones you've added yourself and represent pages visited over many surfing experiences, not just the most recent one.

To select a page from your bookmark list, pull down the **Bookmark/ Favorites** menu and click on the desired entry. In Netscape Communicator, clicking on the **Add Bookmark** command makes a bookmark entry for the current page. **Add to Favorites** performs the same function in Microsoft Internet Explorer.

To save a favorite page location, use the **Add** feature available on both browsers. Clicking that feature adds the location of the current page to your **Bookmark/Favorites** menu. A cautionary note is in order here. Your bookmark or favorites list physically exists only on your personal computer, which means that if you connect to the Internet on a different computer, your list won't be available. If you routinely connect to the Internet from a computer lab, for example, get ready to carry the URLs for your favorite Web sites in your notebook or your head.

part

1

Searching and Search Engines

Returning to our cable television analogy, you may recall that we conveniently glossed over the question of how we selected a starting channel in the first place. With a million TV channels, or several million Web pages, we can't depend solely on luck guiding us to something interesting.

On the Web, we solve the problem with specialized computer programs called *search engines* that crawl through the Web, page by page, cataloging its contents. As different software designers developed search strategies, entrepreneurs established Web sites where any user could find pages containing particular words and phrases. Today, Web sites such as Yahoo!, AltaVista, Excite, WebCrawler, and MetaCrawler offer you a "front door" to the Internet that begins with a search for content of interest.

The URLs for some popular search sites are:

Excite	`www.excite.com`
Yahoo!	`www.yahoo.com`
AltaVista	`www.altavista.digital.com`
WebCrawler	`www.webcrawler.com`
MetaCrawler	`www.metacrawler.com`
Infoseek	`www.infoseek.com`
EBlast	`www.eblast.com`
HotBot	`www.hotbot.com`

Internet Gold Is Where You Find It

Let's perform a simple search using HotBot to find information about the history of the Internet.

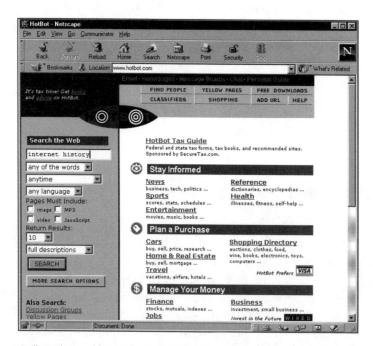

We'll start by searching for the words "internet" or "history." By looking for "any of the words," the search will return pages on which either "internet" or "history" or both appear.

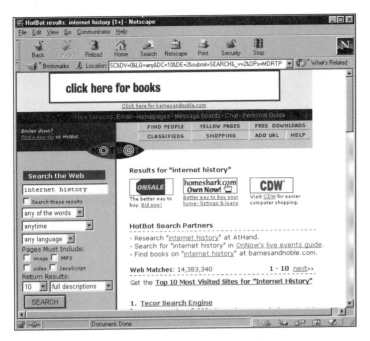

Our search returned 14,383,340 matches or *hits.* Note that the first item doesn't seem to be Internet history–related. By viewing the percentage number in the last line of each summary, you will be able to see the "quality" of the match, which is usually related to the number of times the search word(s) appears on the page.

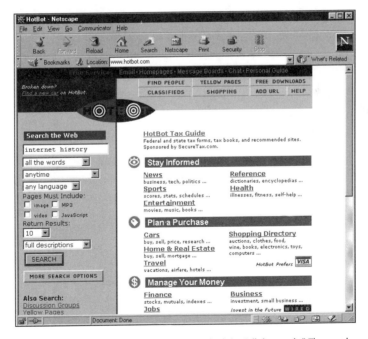

We can conduct the same search, but this time look for "all the words." The search will return hits when both "internet" and "history" appear on the same page, in any order, and not necessarily next to each other.

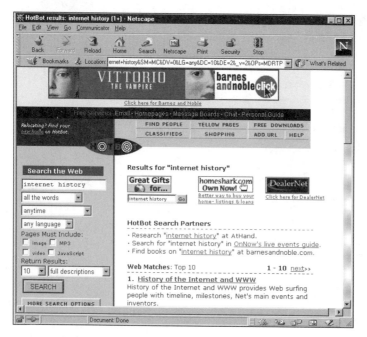

The search is narrowed down somewhat, but it is still not providing us with the information we need.

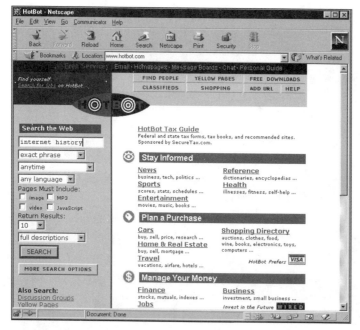

When we search for the exact phrase "internet history," which means those two words in exactly that order, with no intervening words, we're down to about 6,000 hits (still a substantial number).

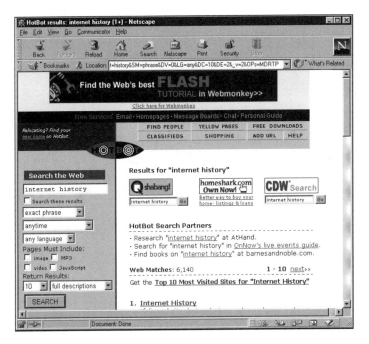

As you can see, the first hit seems to be more specific. However, other hits in the list may have nothing to do with the history of the Internet. Hits happen. No search engine is 100 percent accurate 100 percent of the time. Spurious search results are the serendipity of the Internet. Look at them as an opportunity to explore something new.

Out of curiosity, let's try our history of the Internet search using a different search engine. When we search for the phrase "history of the internet" using WebCrawler, the quotation marks serve the same purpose as selecting "the exact phrase" option in Hotbot. The WebCrawler search only finds 504 hits. Some are the same as those found using HotBot, some are different. Different searching strategies and software algorithms make using more than one search engine a must for serious researchers.

The major search engines conveniently provide you with tips to help you get the most out of their searches. These include ways to use AND and OR to narrow down searches, and ways to use NOT to eliminate unwanted hits.

Each search engine also uses a slightly different approach to cataloging the Web, so at different sites your results might vary. Often, one search engine provides better results (more relevant hits) in your areas of interest; sometimes, the wise strategy is to provide the same input to several different engines. No one search engine does a perfect job all the time, so experience will dictate the one that's most valuable for you.

You'll find search tip pages like this at all the major search engine sites.

Quick Check

Let's review our searching strategies:

- Visit one of the search engine sites;
- Enter key words or phrases that best describe the search criteria;
- Narrow the search if necessary by using options such as "all the words" or "the exact phrase." On some search engines, you may use the word "and" or the symbol "|" to indicate words that all must appear on a page;
- Try using the same criteria with different search engines.

How Not to Come Down with a Virus

Downloading files from the Internet allows less responsible Net citizens to unleash onto your computer viruses, worms, and Trojan horses, all dangerous programs that fool you into thinking they're doing one thing while they're actually erasing your hard disk or performing some other undesirable task. Protection is your responsibility.

One way to reduce the risk of contracting a virus is to download software from reliable sites. Corporations such as Microsoft and Apple take care to make sure downloadable software is virus free. So do most institutions that provide software downloads as a public service (such as the Stanford University archives of Macintosh software). Be especially careful of programs you find on someone's home page. If you're not sure about safe download sources, ask around in a newsgroup (discussed shortly), talk to friends, or check with the information technology center on campus.

You can also buy and use a reliable virus program. Norton, Symantec, and Dr. Solomon all sell first-rate programs for the Mac and PC. You can update these programs right from the Internet so they'll detect the most current viruses. Most of the time, these programs can disinfect files/documents on your disk that contain viruses. Crude as it may sound, downloading programs from the Internet without using a virus check is like having unprotected sex with a stranger. While downloading software may not be life threatening, imagine the consequences if your entire hard disk, including all your course work and software, is totally obliterated. It won't leave you feeling very good.

part

1

If you'd like some entertaining practice sharpening your Web searching skills, point your browser to <www.internettreasurehunt.com>, follow the directions, and you're on your way to becoming an Internet researcher extraordinaire.

The (E)mail Goes Through

Email was one of the first applications created for the Internet by its designers, who sought a method of communicating with each other directly from their keyboards. Your electronic Internet mailbox is to email what a post office box is to "snail mail" (the name Net citizens apply to ordinary, hand-delivered mail). This mailbox resides on the computer of your Internet Service Provider (ISP). That's the organization providing you with your Internet account. Most of the time your ISP will be your school; but, you may contract with one of the commercial providers, such as America Online, Netcom, Microsoft Network, Earthlink, or AT&T. The Internet doesn't deliver a message to your door but instead leaves it in a conveniently accessible place (your mailbox) in the post office (the computer of your ISP), until you retrieve the mail using your combination (password).

If you currently have computer access to the Internet, your school or ISP assigned you a *user name* (also called a user id, account name, or account number). This user name may be your first name, your first initial and the first few characters of your last name, or some strange combination of numbers and letters only a computer could love. An email address is a combination of your user name and the unique address of the computer through which you access your email, like this:

        username@computername.edu

The three letters after the dot, in this case "edu," identify the top level "domain." There are six common domain categories in use: edu (educational), com (commercial), org (organization), net (network), mil (military), and gov (government). The symbol "@"—called the "at" sign in typewriter days—serves two purposes: For computers, it provides a neat, clean separation between your user name and the computer name; for people, it makes Internet addresses more pronounceable. Your address is read: user name "at" computer name "dot" e-d-u. Suppose your Internet user name is "a4736g" and your ISP is Allyn & Bacon, the publisher of this book. Your email address might look like

        a4736g@abacon.com

and you would tell people your email address is "ay-four-seven-three-six-gee at ay bacon dot com."

part

1

We Don't Just Handle Your Email, We're Also a Client

You use email with the aid of special programs called *mail clients*. As with search engines, mail clients have the same set of core features, but your access to these features varies with the type of program. On both the PC and the Mac, Netscape Communicator and Microsoft Internet Explorer give you access to mail clients while you're plugged into the Web. That way you can pick up and send mail while you're surfing the Web.

The basic email service functions are creating and sending mail, reading mail, replying to mail, and forwarding mail. First we'll examine the process of sending and reading mail, and then we'll discuss how to set up your programs so that your messages arrive safely.

Let's look at a typical mail client screen, in this case from Netscape Communicator 4.5. You reach this screen by choosing **Messenger** from under the **Communicator** menu. To send a message from scratch, choose the **New Msg** button to create a blank message form, which has fields for the recipient's address and the subject, and a window for the text of the message.

Fill in the recipient's address in the "To" field, just above the arrow. Use your own address. We'll send email to ourselves and use the same

part

1

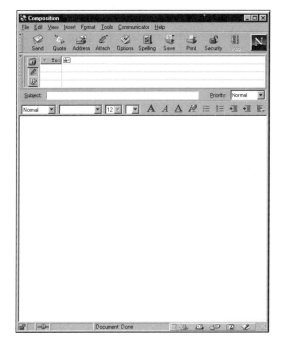

New message form, with fields for recipient's address and the subject, and a window for the text of the message.

message to practice sending email and reading it as well; then we'll know if your messages come out as expected.

Click in the "Subject" field and enter a word or phrase that generally describes the topic of the message. Since we're doing this for the first time, let's type "Maiden Email Voyage."

Now click anywhere in the text window and enter your message. Let's say "Hi. Thanks for guiding me through sending my first email." You'll find that the mail client works here like a word processing program, which means you can insert and delete words and characters and highlight text.

Now click the **Send** button on the Navigation toolbar. You've just created and sent your first email message. In most systems, it takes a few seconds to a few minutes for a message to yourself to reach your mailbox, so you might want to take a short break before continuing. When you're ready to proceed, close the **Composition** window and click the **Get Msg** button.

part

1

What Goes Around Comes Around

Now let's grab hold of the message you just sent to yourself. When retrieving mail, most mail clients display a window showing the messages in your mailbox telling you how many new messages have been added.

If you've never used your email before, chances are your message window is empty, or contains only one or two messages (usually official messages from the ISP) besides the one you sent to yourself. The message to yourself should be accompanied by an indicator of some sort—a colored mark, the letter N—indicating it's a new message. In Netscape Communicator, as in other mail clients, you also get to see the date of the message, who sent it, and the information you entered in the subject line. The Subject field lets you scan your messages and determine which ones you want to look at first.

The summary of received messages tells you everything you need to know about a message except what's in it. Click anywhere in the line to see the contents in the message window. Click on the message from yourself and you'll see the contents of the message displayed in a window. The information at the top—To, From, Subject, and so forth—is called the *header*. Depending on your system, you may also see some cryptic lines with terms such as X-Mailer, received by, and id number. Most of the time, there's nothing in this part of the header of interest, so just skip over it for now.

Moving Forward

The contents, or text, of your message can be cut and pasted just like any other text document. If you and a classmate are working on a project together, your partner can write part of a paper and email it to you, and you can copy the text from your email message and paste it into your word processing program.

What if there are three partners in this project? One partner sends you a draft of the paper for you to review. You like it and want to send it on to your other partner. The **Forward** feature lets you send the message intact, so you don't have to cut and paste it into a new message window. To forward a message, highlight it in the **Inbox** (top) and click the **Forward** icon. Enter the recipient's address in the "To" field of the message window. Note that the subject of the message is "Fwd:" followed by the subject of the original message. Use the text window to add your comments ahead of the original message.

A Chance to Reply

part

1

Email is not a one-way message system. Let's walk through a reply to a message from a correspondent named Elliot. Highlight the message in your **Inbox** again and this time click on the **Reply** icon. When the message window appears, click on the **Quote** icon. Depending on which program you're using, you'll see that each line in the message is preceded by either a vertical bar or a right angle bracket (>).

Note the vertical line to the left of the original text. The "To" and "Subject" fields are filled in automatically with the address of the sender and the original subject preceded by "Re:". In Internet terminology, the message has been *quoted*. The vertical bar or > is used to indicate lines not written by you but by someone else (in this case, the message's original author). Why bother? Because this feature allows you to reply without retyping the parts of the message you're responding to. Because your typing isn't quoted, your answers stand out from the original message. Netscape Communicator 4.5 adds some blank lines above and below your comments, a good practice for you if your mail client doesn't do this automatically.

Welcome to the Internet, Miss Manners

While we're on the subject of email, here are some *netiquette* (net etiquette) tips.

■ When you send email to someone, even someone who knows you well, all they have to look at are your words—there's no body language attached. That means there's no smile, no twinkle in the eye, no raised eyebrow; and especially, there's no tone of voice. What you write is open to interpretation and your recipient has nothing to guide him or her. You may understand the context of a remark, but will your reader? If you have any doubts about how your message will be interpreted, you might want to tack on an *emoticon* to your message. An emoticon is a face created out of keyboard characters. For example, there's the happy Smiley :-) (you have to look at it sideways . . . the parenthesis is its mouth), the frowning Smiley :-((Frownie?), the winking Smiley ;-), and so forth. Smileys are the body language of the Internet. Use them to put remarks in context. "Great," in response to a friend's suggestion means you like the idea. "Great :-(" changes the meaning to one of disappointment or sarcasm. (Want a complete list of emoticons? Try using "emoticon" as a key word for a Web search.)

part
1

■ Keep email messages on target. One of the benefits of email is its speed. Reading through lengthy messages leaves the reader wondering when you'll get to the point.

■ Email's speed carries with it a certain responsibility. Its ease of use and the way a messages seems to cry out for an answer both encourage quick responses, but quick doesn't necessarily mean thoughtful. Once you hit the **Send** icon, that message is gone. There's no recall button. Think before you write, lest you feel the wrath of the modern-day version of your parents' adage: Answer in haste, repent at leisure.

Keeping Things to Yourself

Here's another tip cum cautionary note, this one about Web security. Just as you take care to protect your wallet or purse while walking down a crowded street, it's only good practice to exercise caution with information you'd like to keep (relatively) private. Information you pass around the Internet is stored on, or passed along by, computers that are accessible to others. Although computer system administrators take great care to insure the security of this information, no scheme is completely infallible. Here are some security tips:

- Exercise care when sending sensitive information such as credit card numbers, passwords, even telephone numbers and addresses in plain email. Your email message may pass through four or five computers en route to its destination, and at any of these points, it can be intercepted and read by someone other than the recipient.

- Send personal information over the Web only if the page is secure. Web browsers automatically encrypt information on secure pages, and the information can only be unscrambled at the Web site that created the secure page. You can tell if a page is secure by checking the status bar at the bottom of your browser's window for an icon of a closed lock.

- Remember that any files you store on your ISP's computer are accessible to unscrupulous hackers.

- Protect your password. Many Web client programs, such as mail clients, have your password for you. That means anyone with physical access to your computer can read your email. With a few simple tools, someone can even steal your password. Never leave your password on a lab computer. (Make sure the **Remember Password** or **Save Password** box is unchecked in any application that asks for your password.)

part
1

The closed lock icon in the lower left-hand corner of your browser window indicates a "secure" Web page.

An Audience Far Wider Than You Imagine

Remember that the Web in particular and the Internet in general are communications mediums with a far-reaching audience, and placing information on the Internet is tantamount to publishing it. Certainly, the contents of any message or page you post become public information, but in a newsgroup (an electronic bulletin board), your email address also becomes public knowledge. On a Web page, posting a photo of your favorite music group can violate the photographer's copyright, just as if you published the image in a magazine. Use common sense about posting information you or someone else expects to remain private; and, remember, information on the Web can and will be read by people with different tastes and sensitivities. The Web tends to be self-censoring, so be prepared to handle feedback, both good and bad.

A Discussion of Lists

There's no reason you can't use email to create a discussion group. You pose a question, for example, by sending an email message to everyone in the group. Somebody answers and sends the answer to everyone else on the list, and so on.

At least, that's the theory.

In practice, this is what often happens. As people join and leave the group, you and the rest of your group are consumed with updating your lists, adding new names and deleting old ones. As new people join, their addresses may not make it onto the lists of all the members of the group, so different participants get different messages. The work of administering the lists becomes worse than any value anyone can get out of the group, and so it quickly dissolves.

Generally, you're better off letting the computer handle discussion group administration. A *list server* is a program for administering emailing lists. It automatically adds and deletes list members and handles the distribution of messages.

part

1

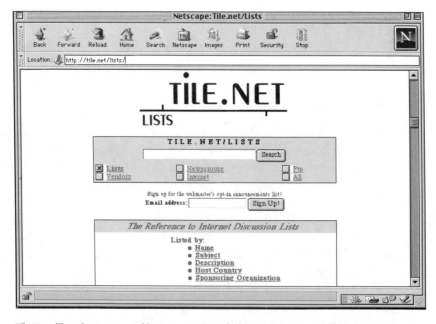

Tile.Net offfers shortcuts to working your way through the Internet's maze of discussion lists.

Thousands of mailing lists have already been formed by users with common interests. You may find mailing lists for celebrities, organizations, political interests, occupations, and hobbies. Your instructor may establish a mailing list for your course.

Groups come in several different flavors. Some are extremely active. You can receive as many as forty or more email messages a day. Other lists may send you a message a month. One-way lists, such as printed newsletters, do not distribute your reply to any other subscriber. Some lists distribute replies to everyone. These lists include mediated lists, in which an "editor" reviews each reply for suitability (relevance, tone, use of language) before distributing the message, and unmediated lists, in which each subscriber's response is automatically distributed to all the other subscribers with no restrictions except those dictated by decency and common sense, though these qualities may not always be obvious from reading the messages.

Get on a List Online

You join in the discussion by subscribing to a list, which is as straightforward as sending email. You need to know only two items: the name of the list and the address of the list server program handling subscriptions. To join a list, send a **Subscribe** message to the list server address. The message must contain the letters "Sub," the name of the list, and your name (your real name, not your user name), all on one line. *And that's all.* This message will be read by a computer program that looks for these items only. At the very best, other comments in the message will be ignored. At the very worst, your entire message will be ignored, and so will you.

Within a few hours to a day after subscribing, the list server will automatically send you a confirmation email message, including instructions for sending messages, finding out information about the list and its members, and canceling your subscription. Save this message for future reference. That way, if you do decide to leave the list, you won't have to circulate a message to the members asking how to unsubscribe, and you won't have to wade through fifty replies all relaying the same information you received when you joined.

Soon after your confirmation message appears in your mailbox, and depending on the activity level of the list, you'll begin receiving email messages. New list subscribers customarily wait a while before joining the discussion. After all, you're electronically strolling into a room full of strangers; it's only fair to see what topics are being discussed before

part
1

wading in with your own opinions. Otherwise, you're like the bore at the party who elbows his way into a conversation with "But enough about you, let's talk about me." You'll also want to avoid the faux pas of posting a long missive on a topic that subscribers spent the preceding three weeks thrashing out. Observe the list for a while, understand its tone and feel, what topics are of interest to others and what areas are taboo. Also, look for personalities. Who's the most vociferous? Who writes very little but responds thoughtfully? Who's the most flexible? The most rigid? Most of all, keep in mind that there are far more observers than participants. What you write may be read by 10 or 100 times more people than those whose names show up in the daily messages.

When you reply to a message, you reply to the list server address, not to the address of the sender (unless you intend for your communication to remain private). The list server program takes care of distributing your message listwide. Use the address in the "Reply To" field of the message. Most mail clients automatically use this address when you select the **Reply** command. Some may ask if you want to use the reply address (say yes). Some lists will send a copy of your reply to you so you know your message is online. Others don't send the author a copy, relying on your faith in the infallibility of computers.

In the words of those famous late night television commercials, you can cancel your subscription at any time. Simply send a message to the address you used to subscribe (which you'll find on that confirmation message you saved for reference), with "Unsub," followed on the same line by the name of the list. For example, to leave a list named "WRITER-L," you would send:

```
Unsub WRITER-L
```

Even if you receive messages for a short while afterwards, have faith— they will disappear.

Waste Not, Want Not

List servers create an excellent forum for people with common interests to share their views; however, from the Internet standpoint, these lists are terribly wasteful. First of all, if there are one thousand subscribers to a list, every message must be copied one thousand times and distributed over the Internet. If there are forty replies a day, this one list creates forty thousand email messages. Ten such lists mean almost a half million messages, most of which are identical, flying around the Net.

Another wasteful aspect of list servers is the way in which messages are answered. The messages in your mailbox on any given day represent a combination of new topics and responses to previous messages. But where are these previous messages? If you saved them, they're in your email mailbox taking up disk space. If you haven't saved them, you have nothing to compare the response to. What if a particular message touches off a chain of responses, with subscribers referring not only to the source message but to responses as well? It sounds like the only safe strategy is to save every message from the list, a suggestion as absurd as it is impractical.

What we really need is something closer to a bulletin board than a mailing list. On a bulletin board, messages are posted once. Similar notices wind up clustered together. Everyone comes to the same place to read or post messages.

And Now the News(group)

The Internet equivalent of the bulletin board is the Usenet or newsgroup area. Usenet messages are copied only once for each ISP supporting the newsgroup. If there are one thousand students on your campus reading the same newsgroup message, there need only be one copy of the message stored on your school's computer.

Categorizing a World of Information

Newsgroups are categorized by topics, with topics broken down into subtopics and sub-subtopics. For example, you'll find newsgroups devoted to computers, hobbies, science, social issues, and "alternatives." Newsgroups in this last category cover a wide range of topics that may not appeal to the mainstream. Also in this category are beginning newsgroups.

Usenet names are amalgams of their topics and subtopics, separated by dots. If you were interested in a newsgroup dealing with, say, music, you might start with rec.music and move down to rec.music.radiohead, or rec.music.techno, and so forth. The naming scheme allows you to zero in on a topic of interest.

Getting into the News(group) Business

Most of the work of reading, responding to, and posting messages is handled by a news reader client program, accessible through both Netscape Communicator and Microsoft Internet Explorer. You can not only surf the Web and handle your mail via your browser, but you can also drop into your favorite newsgroups virtually all in one operation.

Let's drop into a newsgroup. To reach groups via Netscape Communicator 4.5, go to the Communicator menu Bar and select **Newsgroups.** Then, from the File menu, select **Subscribe.** A dialogue box will open that displays a list of available groups.

To subscribe to a newsgroup—that is, to tell your news reader you want to be kept up-to-date on the messages posted to a particular group—highlight the group of interest and click on **Subscribe.** Alternately, you can click in the Subscribe column to the right of the group name. The check mark in the Subscribe column means you're "in." Now, click **OK.**

The message center in Netscape Communicator displays a list of newsgroups on your subscription list. Double click on the one of current interest and your reader presents you with a list of messages posted on the group's bulletin board. Double click on a message to open its contents in a window.

Often, messages contain "Re:" in their subject lines, indicating a response to a previous message (the letters stand for "Regarding"). Many news readers maintain a *thread* for you. Threads are chains of messages and all responses to that message. These readers give you the option to read messages chronologically or to read a message followed by its responses.

When you subscribe to a newsgroup, your news reader will also keep track of the messages you've read so that it can present you with the newest (unread) ones. While older messages are still available to you, this feature guarantees that you stay up-to-date without any record keeping on your part. Subscribing to a newsgroup is free, and the subscription information resides on your computer.

Newsgroups have no way of knowing who their subscribers are, and the same caveat that applies to bookmarks applies to newsgroups. Information about your subscriptions resides physically on the personal computer you're using. If you switch computers, as in a lab, your subscription information and history of read messages are beyond your reach.

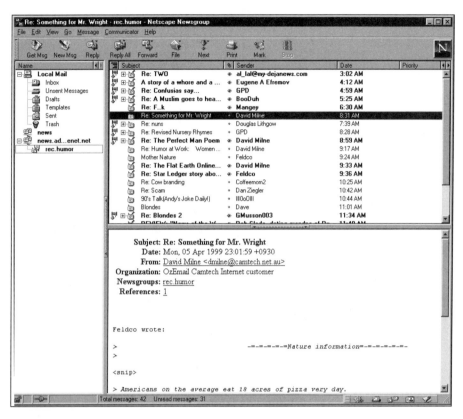

part
1

The top part of this figure shows a listing of posted messages. While not visible from this black and white reproduction, a red indicator in the Subject column marks unread messages. Double-clicking on a message opens its contents into a window shown in the bottom part of this figure. You can reply to this message via the Reply icon, or get the next message using the Next icon.

Welcome to the Internet, Miss Manners—Again

As with list servers, hang out for a while, or *lurk,* to familiarize yourself with the style, tone, and content of newsgroup messages. As you probably surmised from the names of the groups, their topics of discussion are quite narrow. One of the no-nos of newsgroups is posting messages on subjects outside the focus of the group. Posting off-topic messages, especially lengthy ones, is an excellent way to attract a flaming.

A *flame* is a brutally debasing message from one user to another. Flames are designed to hurt and offend, and often the target of the flame feels compelled to respond in kind to protect his or her self-esteem. This leads to a *flame war,* as other users take sides and wade in with flames of their own. If you find yourself the target of a flame, your best strategy is to ignore it. As with a campfire, if no one tends to the flames, they soon die out.

As mentioned earlier, posting messages to newsgroups is a modern form of publishing, and a publisher assumes certain responsibilities. You have a duty to keep your messages short and to the point. Many newsgroup visitors connect to the Internet via modems. Downloading a day's worth of long postings, especially uninteresting ones, is annoying and frustrating. Similarly, don't post the same message to multiple, re-lated newsgroups. This is called *cross posting,* and it's a peeve of Net citizens who check into these groups. If you've ever flipped the television from channel to channel during a commercial break only to encounter the same commercial (an advertising practice called *roadblocking*), you can imagine how annoying it is to drop in on several newsgroups only to find the same messages posted to each one.

part

1

With the huge potential audience newsgroups offer, you might think you've found an excellent medium for advertising goods or services. After all, posting a few messages appears analogous to running classified ads in newspapers, only here the cost is free. There's a name for these kinds of messages—*spam.* Spam is the junk mail of the Internet, and the practice of spamming is a surefire way to attract flames. The best advice for handling spam? Don't answer it. Not only does an answer encourage the spammer, but he or she will also undoubtedly put your email address on a list and sell it to other spammers, who will flood your online mail-box with their junk.

Above all, be considerate of others. Treat them the way you'd like to be treated. Do you enjoy having your grammar or word choices cor-rected in front of the whole world? Do you feel comfortable when some-one calls you stupid in public? Do you appreciate having your religion, ethnicity, heritage, or gender belittled in front of an audience? Respect the rights and feelings of others, if not out of simple decency then out of the sanctions your ISP may impose. Although you have every right to ex-press an unpopular opinion or to take issue with the postings of others, most ISPs have regulations about the kinds of messages one can send via their facilities. Obscenities, threats, and spam may, at a minimum, result in your losing your Internet access privileges.

Give Your Web Browser Some Personality—Yours

Before accessing email and newsgroup functions, you need to set up or personalize your browser. If you always work on the same personal computer, this is a one-time operation that takes only a few minutes. In it, you tell your browser where to find essential computer servers, along with personal information the Internet needs to move messages for you.

- *Step 1:* Open the **Preferences** menu in Netscape or the **Internet Options** in Internet Explorer. In Netscape Communicator the Preferences menu is located under the **Edit** menu; in Microsoft Internet Explorer the Internet Options can be found under the **View** menu.

- *Step 2:* Tell the browser who you are and where to find your mail servers. Your Reply To address is typically the same as your email address, though if you have an email alias you can use it here. Microsoft Internet Explorer has slots for your mail servers in the same window. Your ISP will provide the server names and addresses. Be sure to use your user name (and not your alias) in the "Account Name" field. SMTP handles your outgoing messages, while the POP3 server routes incoming mail. Often, but not always, these server names are the same. Netscape Communicator has a separate window for server names.

- *Step 3:* Tell the browser where to find your news server. Your ISP will furnish the name of the server. Note that in Microsoft Internet Explorer, you specify a helper application to read the news. Now that most computers come with browsers already loaded onto the hard disk, you'll find that these helper applications are already set up for you.

- *Step 4:* Set your home page. For convenience, you may want your browser to start by fetching a particular page, such as your favorite search site. Or you might want to begin at your school library's home page. Enter the URL for this starting page in the home page address field. Both Netscape and Microsoft offer the option of no home page when you start up. In that case, you get a blank browser window.

Operating systems such as Mac OS 8 and Microsoft Windows 95 offer automated help in setting up your browsers for Web, mail, and

part

1

newsgroup operation. You need to know the names of the servers mentioned above, along with your user name and other details, such as the address of the domain name server (DNS) of your ISP. You should receive all this information when you open your Internet account. If not, ask for it.

Speech Communication on the Internet

The Internet offers unimaginable potential for information, and now you have access to it. What can you do?

As a student of communication, consider the various ways that you can use the Internet to achieve communication goals: Is your goal to relate to someone? To gather information, or to present an informative or persuasive message? Do you want to be a participant in a communication situation as an audience member? Do you want to directly interact with another Internet user? When you get on the Internet, you can achieve any of these goals. For the Internet is a unique channel of communication for relating to people (similar to letter writing or the telephone), as a medium of expression (like owning your own newspaper or radio station), and as a place where you can go to participate as an audience member (akin to listening to the radio or watching television). Yet, the personal computer, connected to the Internet, is more than any one of these traditional communication venues; when we connect with one another using the conventions of multimedia, it becomes an integration of all of them.

In the last section we looked at two simple ways to communicate by using email and participating in discussion groups. In this section, we will explore some further ways that you can use the World Wide Web and incorporate emerging multimedia technologies.

Using the Internet to Relate

Before talking about the mechanics of connecting to people by way of the Internet, let's consider why you would want to relate to other people through the Net. Probably for the same reasons that people relate to one another in every day face-to-face communication, because you share common interests; you need information; or you have a message you

part

1

want to share. As a public speaking student you may want to bounce your ideas off of a receptive and interested listener, or get advice and evidence to use in your speech.

Use the Web To Participate in a Usenet Discussion Group

Your Web browser can take the place of a news reader. And though it may not be as useful as one of the more sophisticated news readers that afford you options for organizing and searching the Web, employing your browser as a point of contact saves you the effort of setting up a separate news reader.

How do you find a Usenet group? It is actually a whole lot easier than finding an email address. The simplest search method is to use Search Engines on the World Wide Web. Earlier, we looked at how you use these to find Web pages. Now let's try out two search engines that can also locate Usenet groups that fit your needs: AltaVista and DejaNews.

1. First, try AltaVista. Its URL is http://www.altavista.digital.com/. Recall how it does keyword searches. AltaVista will search through Usenet and find postings that deal with your keyword.

2. Note in AltaVista how you can designate that you want it to search web pages or Usenet groups. We are going to select "Usenet." You should be able to find the input box to select Usenet at the top, just below the AltaVista banner.

3. Type in the search string "death penalty" and hit ENTER on your keyboard or mouse click on the button marked "Search."

4. The outcome of the search is a table with a list of recent postings. First, you'll see the date of a post, then the Usenet group on which the postings were made such as misc.legal. You will next see the email address for a participant. On many Web browsers, clicking on the person's email address will open your mail client and allow you to send an email message—not a Usenet posting—to the person. Unless it is your intention to communicate directly with the person, don't click it. Rather, you want to click on the posting itself. It will most likely begin with the omnipresent Re: that identifies it as a response to a whole string of earlier posts. Click on the that line, and you will go to the Usenet discussion itself.

5. From AltaVista, you are simply a "lurker" in the discussion; you can't enter into the fray. For that, we'll need a different Web address.

part

1

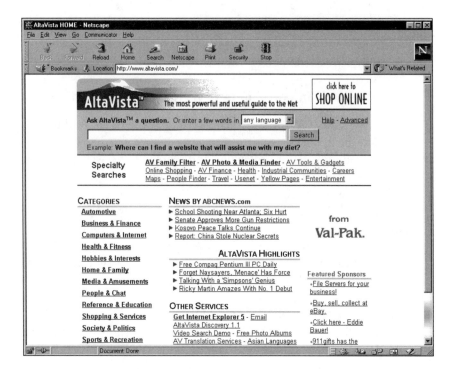

To be a more active participant in Usenet, using your Web browser, we'll use DejaNews.

DejaNews emulates a traditional newsreader but uses the familiar page format of the Web. DejaNews calls itself "the source for Internet newsgroups," and that is mostly true, especially insofar as it allows you to find and jump into a newsgroup. Frankly, taking part in Newsgroups can't get any easier! Seasoned Usenet participants will probably want to stick with a newsreader, however, since these utilities often provide many more resources for organizing discussion threads, and allowing you to return easily to the newsgroup day after day.

1. Point your Web browser to the URL http://www.deja.com/.

2. Enter a search string in the box under "Search Deja.com." DejaNews will do a restricted search if you put a phrase in quotation marks. Try typing in "teen smoking." (Remember how we did this in Part I using AltaVista; it's the same technique to limit the number of post-ings just to those that relate to teen smoking alone, thus leaving out the numerous other references to teenagers or to smoking.) You can search for discussion groups or posts to discussion groups by select-

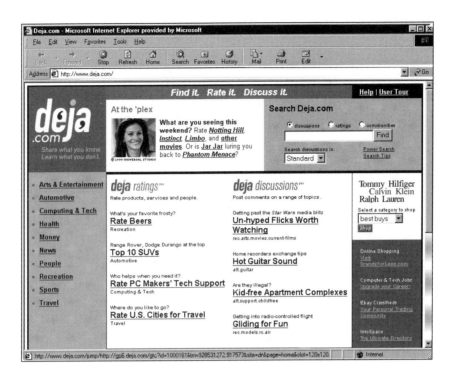

ing "discussions." After you have selected "discussions," click the "Find" button.

3. The same information we found on the AltaVista list is present here, but in a different order. First, you see the date of the posting. Then, the "Subject" column identifies the message. Next, you will see the newsgroup, such as alt.smokers. Last in the row is the user ID of a contributor. Click on a hyperlinked subject heading to take you to the message.

4. The author posting history link is useful. Click it and you will see how many postings, and on how many different newsgroups a particular author has weighed in. (It may cause you to wonder if some folks have a life outside of participating in newsgroups!)

5. You also have options to post a reply, send e-mail, mail the message to a friend or subscribe to the discussion group. If you decide to post a reply or article, a form will be provided for you to register as a DejaNews user and to write your reply.

You can find additional resources for participating in Usenet newsgroups at the Allyn and Bacon Public Speaking Website. Go to http://www.abacon.com/pubspeak/research/usezine.html

Browsing vs. Searching

Many times, the best way to find information on the Web is by browsing rather than searching. When you browse, you're not entirely sure just what you are looking for, much as one simply browses in a store wandering among aisles to see what is on the shelves. Tile.Net-News may be a good browsing source for you since it arranges newsgroups and subjects alphabetically.

Just scroll down the alphabetic list and see what is there. The URL for Tile.Net-News is http://tile.net/news/listed.html/.

Many Usenet groups have FAQs (Frequently Asked Questions). These are questions that have been asked so many times by people entering the groups for the first time that users got tired of answering the same questions week after week and compiled the questions and their answers into a list for new users. You should find the FAQs for any group that you want to participate in. They define what the group is about in more detail than the group's name alone would suggest, and they answer many other of the questions that help explain what the group is about and what is considered appropriate and what is not. There is also a Web page for finding FAQs. Try out Usenet FAQs at http://www.cis.ohio-state.edu/hypertext/faq/usenet/FAQ-List.html/.

And now, a caution! Since Usenet is essentially uncontrolled, expect just about any kind of posting. There will be some serious discussions with thoughtful and respectful opinions and lots of good useful information. And, particularly but not exclusively in the alt groups, there will be trivia, profanity, irrational comments, inexplicable anger, and out-and-out wrong information. If you're easily offended, beware; and if you tend to believe everything you read, you're in for a rude awakening on Usenet. But it's almost always a lively discussion. Remember, too, you are probably using discussion groups as a way of exploring ideas; don't expect that all the offerings you receive from a discussion group will constitute solid evidence to use in a speech, though your interactions online may provide you with leads for finding good sources of evidence.

part

1

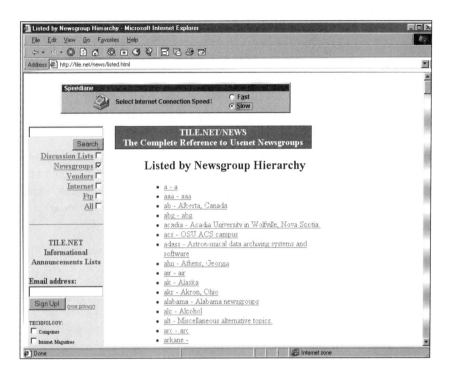

Take Part in a Web Based Forum Through an Organization, Newspaper, or Magazine

First, there was Usenet, which, as we explained above, has been around for several years. Then, came online forums such as the special interest groups on networks like America Online. Both of these preceded the Web. With the development of the World Wide Web, we have a new breed of online forum that is part of a Website.

Web based forums are somewhat akin to Usenet. Posters on the board offer opinions as part of a thread that will look much the same as the thread for a newsgroup. Web based forums differ since they are likely to be accessed from the home page of a Website for the organization or publication that sponsors them. To illustrate how a Web based forum operates, we will go to the Talk Central page at the *Washington Post.*

1. Point your browser to http://www.washingtonpost.com/wp-srv/talk/ front.htm/.

2. Click on one of the chat or discussion topics. You will then learn how to register and participate in online discussions. Registering to

participate in the forum does not require that you subscribe to the Post itself, though you will be asked in the process of your initial registration if you receive a copy of the newspaper. Other information that you will need is a regular address and an email address. You will also be asked to create a password for yourself, and you can elect to enter that password for each subsequent visit that you make to Talk Central or have it stored on your system.

3. Go back to Talk Central by clicking the link to return to the forum, choose "Open Forum" under the headings of International or National News. These provide the greatest range of topic areas. As you scroll down, you can see the way various topics are arrayed in a hierarchy.

4. When you click on a thread, you will be able to see each of the entries in the thread arranged in reverse chronological order.

5. At the end of the thread, find the option for expressing your own opinion. Note how you type in your response in a box. Then click on "Add my Note." Come back in a day or two to see if anyone has responded to your message.

So, how do you find these new forums? One of the most useful search tools for finding online discussions is Forum One. It indexes over 200,000 different online groups.

1. Point your browser to http://www.forumone.com/. Look for the familiar search form so that you can enter your terms. Try "campaign finance reform." (Note the use of the terms in quotation marks in order to confine the search.)

2. Forum One will probably find several discussions. It will also identify the sponsoring organization or publication and indicate if you need to be a registered participant. Usually to register, you need to provide an email address and a password. It is often useful to have a password in mind; keep it simple so that you can remember it when you return. Sometimes, you may have to acknowledge reading the guidelines and policies of the group. It's a matter of Netiquette.

3. Join one of the discussion groups. Then, navigate your way around based on what you have learned already.

You can find out more about online discussion groups by using a special page on the Allyn and Bacon Public Speaking Website. This page

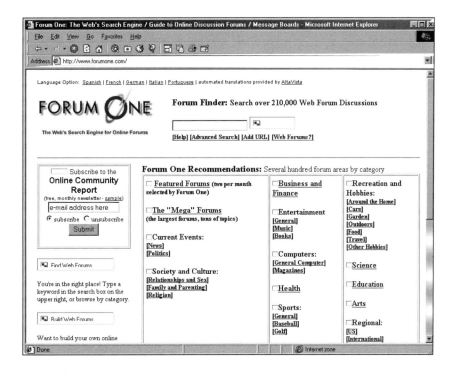

lists a variety of types of online forums. Go to http://www.abacon.com/pubspeak/assess/netforum.html#ab/.

Online Chat—Live

One of the newest features in the current year is live chat by way of a Web browser. Longtime AOL users or veterans of dial-up bulletin boards have done BBS style chatting for a number of years. Unlike Usenet or email discussion groups whose participants communicate in asynchronous time, online chat occurs in synchronous time. It is as close to face-to-face conversation as one can get, for you are interacting in real time, sending messages and receiving feedback immediately! Your messages to and fro are typed in on the keyboard; we'll look more at audio and video chat later under the multimedia section.

To try Web based chat, first locate a live chat room. Yahoo Chat Events provides a convenient list, and identifies times for chat. Go to http://events.yahoo.com/. Try it out. You will see a broad range of topic areas. Once you select your topic, you will be linked to the page that sponsors the chat, and learn the ropes for taking part.

Another venue for finding and participating in Web based chat is Excite.

1. First, get there by going to http://www.excite.com/channel/chat/.

2. Notice how the chat area is set up. In the right hand column are Bulletin Boards on a variety of subjects. These are asynchronous; you post a message at one point in time, and someone else responds at a later time. We're going to focus on the second column, labeled "Chat Events." You may need to scroll down the page where you will see live events listed by time. When you click on one of the chat topics, you will next be taken to a page for downloading the chat software used on Excite.

3. Excite will tell you how many people are in the chat area. If you click on the Live Chat link you will add another number to the total. Observe that they offer further advice on how to take part.

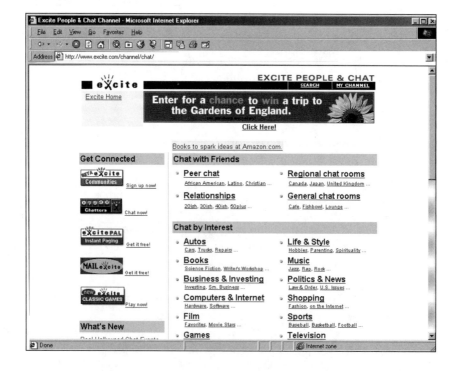

You can also find a listing of live chat rooms on the Allyn and Bacon Public Speaking Website at http://www.abacon.com/pubspeak/assess/viraud.html/.

Now that you can see how you can interact with people through online discussions in various venues such as Usenet, forums, and chat, we will turn next to how you can present some of your ideas on a Web page that uses multimedia features.

Multimedia and the Internet

What is meant by the term multimedia? Ask experts on the subject and you'll receive a range of answers. But, all seem to boil it down to the idea of **integration**. A page on the Web integrates text, sound, visual materials and opportunities for you, the user, to interact. Interaction means that audio and visual information can be linked together in ways that allow the user to navigate through layers of related information.

Many online learning experiences expose us to information presented in radically different ways. Because information on the Web is presented associatively (linking related concepts together) and not in linear or chronological ways, you become an active agent of the communication process. You are not simply a passive reader or TV couch potato, but a co-creator of the form.

Moreover, when you write your own Web page, you can communicate your ideas with multimedia elements that allow you to engage your audience. Think of it as an opportunity to provide a creative experience for your audience, as well.

part

1

Setting Up Your Own Home Page on the Web

In this part we will start by looking at the three-step process of creating a Web page. Then, we will consider some examples of types of interactive multimedia experiences that you can participate in as virtual speaking situations.

The First Step Is Planning and Designing the Page

Like any creative process, this first step will require answering some critical questions: Why do you want a Web page? What do you want to say? What links, text, graphics, sound, video, etc., would you like to include?

There are a few rules of thumb that other people have established about creating Web pages:

Be sparing with text. Long text passages are difficult and tiresome to read on a computer screen. You should try to make sure your viewer doesn't have to scroll through more than one or two screens of text. If you have a long textual passage, consider how the information can be organized into manageable chunks. Use bookmarks that enable the reader to jump back and forth from a table of contents at the top of the page to the blocks of information that follow.

Keep the graphics as small as you can. Beautiful graphics files that are fifty or 100K will take too long to load. A good rule of thumb to follow is to keep all of the graphics combined within a limit of 30K per page. There are two graphic formats used on the Web: GIF files, and JPEG. You may find it useful to get a graphics program that allows you to convert files or reduce the color resolution of your images. Adobe Photoshop is one of the standards in the field. Another program, which is a reasonably inexpensive shareware program, is Paint Shop Pro. You can even download PSP from its creator JASC by going to their Website: http://www.jasc.com/index.html. After you've tried the program for thirty days, you ought to pay the shareware fee or uninstall it from your system.

Keep multimedia files small. The principle of maintaining a small file size fits for sound, video, or animation files, as well. Even when your audience member has a sophisticated machine, a state of the art browser, and uses the fastest modem speed, files still take a long time to load. Look into sound formats that compress. For instance, True Speech, developed by DSP and native to the current Windows platforms (though it can be used on other operating systems as well) significantly conserves file size. If you are going to talk on your Web page, convert your files to True Speech. You can download the necessary software to use along with your soundcard from DSP at http://www.dspg.com/player/main.htm.

Microsoft's PowerPoint Animation Viewer for Active X can be used to create excellent animations that are much smaller than the normal .avi file. If you have PowerPoint 7.0 and use Windows 95, download the animation software from http://www.microsoft.com/msdownload/.

part

1

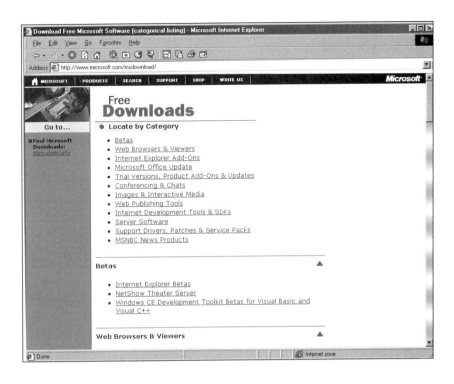

If one uses Astound, another presentation package, you can download its new WebMotion program. Astound does file compression very effectively. Get it at http://www.astound.com/.

Develop a consistent layout. Don't use a radically different page layout for each page in your site. If you change background styles or have a significantly different setup for a page, there ought to be a reason for that change. Does the change fit the mood you are establishing? Does the new page present an entirely different variety of information?

Help your audience get back to the main home page. It is also very important to have a title for each page since it allows the audience member to bookmark the page more easily if he or she wants to return to it another time.

Include a way for people to contact you. You can provide an email address or a tag that allows the viewer to send you email.

Second, You Need To Actually Make the Files That Are the Web Site

This involves actually taking the information you want to include and writing the html code. (The acronym html stands for hypertext markup language.) There are numerous guides to HTML authoring available on-line. One of the best is *A Beginner's Guide to HTML,* located at http://www.ncsa.uiuc.edu/General/Internet/WWW/HTMLPrimer.html. More advanced users might turn to *The Bare Bones Guide to HTML* by Kevin Werbach since it includes more sophisticated HTML specifications and explains Netscape extensions. You can find it at http://werbach.com/barebones.

But the easiest way to actually create the files needed for your Web page is to use a software application such as Adobe PageMill or Claris Home Page (for both Macintosh and Windows) that gives you a nearly WYSIWIG (What You See Is What You Get . . . well sort of) approach to Web page creation. In addition to the programs specifically designed for making home pages, you can use one of the major office suites (Microsoft Word, Corel's WordPerfect, ClarisWorks, etc.). Each of these has built-in routines to allow you to convert a word processing file into an HTML file. With such programs, you compose your text, add your graphics, make your lists and other displays, and the application actually writes the text file with the correct HTML tags embedded already for you. If you have a license for one of these programs, check out your manual to see what kind of Web construction features are available to you, or go to the Web page for the company that produces the software to see if there is a Web editor that you can download.

Third, You Need To Find A Server and Transfer the Files

This entails determining the best location for the site you've created, usually on your school's server or an Internet service provider such as America Online. You may be subject to a number of restrictions, especially if you use your school's server, and you may even have to sign a document attesting that you won't post anything on your individual Web page that could reflect badly on the school. Pornography is almost universally outlawed. Schools may also have guidelines about expressions that are racist, sexist, homophobic, ethnically-prejudiced, or offensive in other ways. You need to consider the type of software needed to upload to the server, and of course, the monthly cost and file capacity for your site.

part

1

Interactivity in Virtual Worlds on the Web

Throughout this unit, we have emphasized the notion of interactivity. On the Web, as you follow the links and paths that *you* want to follow, you are essentially writing your own book of knowledge, not reading someone else's book. When you create a Web page, your audience member interacts with you, and your ideas. We will conclude this section by examining some of the emerging new forms of Web interactivity.

One of the inherent limitations of *writing* is that the static words on a printed page will quickly become out of date. Moreover, as Socrates complained in the dialogue the *Phaedrus,* the reader using printed media cannot talk back to the writer. The emerging form for Web pages is breaking away from the printed page to enable information providers to update their content more quickly and to engage the audience. To see how that occurs, we need to think a bit about where the Web has been, and where it is going. Let's think about three generations of the Web.

The first generation was the *text-based* Web. It presented information as brief paragraphs of information organized by lists of bullets. Interactivity occurred by linking to other pages, and in some situations, it afforded the user options for downloading information from the Web page. Multimedia elements such as graphics and sound were limited, and usually made available as links or downloads.

The second generation has been the *graphical* page. The graphical page embedded visual effects—usually as backgrounds, colors, or GIF and JPEG files that loaded onto the page. The visually enhanced page content remained very similar to the text-based page. Developments like the 2.0 version of Windows Explorer allowed Web designers to embed short .wav sound files or midi files into a page.

The third generation is the *interactive multimedia page.* This page strives to build on the aesthetics of the graphical page to engage the audience by using dynamic audiovisual files. Several new software and programming developments have led to this page.

The first is the concept of "streaming." When a file is streamed it is being loaded as the audience member hears or sees it. Consider this contrast. To place a regular audio file on a page in the second generation, the user would have had to wait for the entire file to be loaded onto the page before hearing it; a streamed file arrives in "packets." As one is hearing the file, more is on the way that you will be hearing momentarily. One of the current technologies for streaming is RealAudio. You can find out more about RealAudio by going to the homepage of its creator, RealNetworks at http://www.realaudio.com/. If you download Real-

part

1

Audio, go next to some of the sites summarized in Section B of Part II as "Live Events." Then, you can "listen" to live events, or hear an audio file as it is being downloaded from an archive. RealAudio enables one to hear radio programming far beyond the reach of your regular radio antenna's power to pick up a signal.

The second development is the "interactive form." One of the forerunners to this was the mailto: code that allows a Web page to open up your email editor so that you can send mail to a Web page author. More sophisticated forms can be tailored for you to enter data in boxes, and then send that information back to the maker.

Some interesting interactive forms allow you to access a database, and even print out a table of information. The Gazetteer from the U.S. Census Bureau is a good example of a page using this tool. You can simply type in your zip code to develop a demographic profile of your community using data from the most recent census. By clicking boxes on the form, you customize the demographic profile by selecting the type of information you want to receive. To use this, go to http://www.census.gov/cgi-bin/gazetteer/.

Another example of a highly interactive page is Project VoteSmart. VoteSmart is a citizens action group that evaluates the performance of members of Congress. From its home page at http://www.vote-smart.org/ you can do a zip code search to find information about your Congressional Representatives and members of the Senate, your State Governor and legislative representatives, and the President, of course. Among the many things you can do from the Project VoteSmart page, you can find out results from a survey on the stands they've taken on various issues (the NPAT Questionnaire that VoteSmart has sends to every elected official or serious candidate), read a biographical sketch, find out how they voted on a range of issues, find out who contributes money to their campaigns, and send an email message.

Interactive pages, increasingly, add a bulletin board or even live chat to a page. You will thus see that many newspapers, magazines, and organizations have created forums in which the user may participate. Some of these rely on the most up-to-date browsers from Microsoft or Netscape so that you can chat without the need for a separate plug-in such as ichat or CuSeeMe.

The third development is compression and streaming of animation files. The newest programming language for integration of animation on pages is Java, which is an object oriented programming language. With it, one may create applets, which are self contained programs that operate when a Web page is loaded. The applet enables the user to do some-

part

1

thing interactively, or it plays the sound or video file. The newest browsers from Netscape and Microsoft enable you to view animated files. Read further about these by going to the respective homepages of Netscape at http://www.netscape.com and Microsoft at http://www.microsoft.com/msdownload/.

Animation is just the start of using dynamic visual effects on a page, the next developments, now quite nascent, are streaming video and virtual reality. Video interaction via the net has been an idea on the boards for a number of years, but the amount of bandwidth for transmitting video images is huge. For now—and it is unfortunately a jerky output—the emerging industry standard is RealVideo from RealNetworks. As we develop larger pipelines and more efficient compression technologies for conveying information over the Internet, we will see more uses of interactive video. Video conferencing over the Net is presently available using CuSeeMe. You can learn more about it at http://www.cu-seeme.net/. You can find out more about virtual reality from the homepage of one of the original thinkers on the subject, Mark Pesce. Go to http://hyperreal.com/~mpesce/. You can also see a sample of VRML coded documents if you go the Microsoft homepage and download its VRML viewer that becomes part of the Windows Explorer Web browser.

What's next? The fifth generation of the Web is not far away, either! Expect to see even greater integration of video and even more active interactivity.

part

1

Critical Evaluation

Where Seeing Is Not Always Believing

Typical research resources, such as journal articles, books, and other scholarly works, are reviewed by a panel of experts before being published. At the very least, any reputable publisher takes care to assure that the author is who he or she claims to be and that the work being published represents a reasoned and informed point of view. When anyone can post anything in a Web site or to a newsgroup, the burden of assessing the relevance and accuracy of what you read falls to you. Rumors quickly grow into facts on the Internet simply because stories can spread so rapidly that the "news" seems to be everywhere. Because the Internet leaves few tracks, in no time it's impossible to tell whether you are reading independent stories or the merely same story that's been around the world two or three times. Gathering information on the Internet may be quick, but verifying the quality of information requires a serious commitment.

Approach researching via the Internet with confidence, however, and not with trepidation. You'll find it an excellent workout for your critical evaluation skills; no matter what career you pursue, employers value an employee who can think critically and independently. Critical thinking is also the basis of problem solving, another ability highly valued by the business community. So, as you research your academic projects, be assured that you're simultaneously developing lifelong expertise.

It's Okay to Be Critical of Others

The first tip for successful researching on the Internet is to always consider your source. A Web site's URL often alerts you to the sponsor of the site. CNN or MSNBC are established news organizations, and you can give the information you find at their sites the same weight you would give to their cablecasts. Likewise, major newspapers operate Web sites with articles reprinted from their daily editions or expanded stories written expressly for the Internet. On the other hand, if you're unfamiliar with the source, treat the information the way you would any new data. Look for specifics—"66 percent of all voters" as opposed to "most voters"—and for information that can be verified—a cited report in another medium or information accessible through a Web site hosted by a credible sponsor—as opposed to generalities or unverifiable claims. Look for independent paths to the same information. This can involve careful use of search engines or visits to newsgroups with both similar and opposing viewpoints. Make sure that the "independent" information you find is truly independent. In newsgroups don't discount the possibility of multiple postings, or that a posting in one group is nothing more than a quotation from a posting in another. Ways to verify independent paths include following sources (if any) back to their origins, contacting the person posting a message and asking for clarification, or checking other media for verification.

In many cases, you can use your intuition and common sense to raise your comfort level about the soundness of the information. With both list servers and newsgroups, it's possible to lurk for a while to develop a feeling for the authors of various postings. Who seems the most authoritarian, and who seems to be "speaking" from emotion or bias? Who seems to know what he or she is talking about on a regular basis? Do these people cite their sources of information (a job or affiliation perhaps)? Do they have a history of thoughtful, insightful postings, or do their postings typically contain generalities, unjustifiable claims, or flames? On Web sites, where the information feels more anonymous, there are also clues you can use to test for authenticity. Verify who's hosting the Web site. If the host or domain name is unfamiliar to you, perhaps a search engine can help you locate more information. Measure the tone and style of the writing at the site. Does it seem consistent with the education level and knowledge base necessary to write intelligently about the subject?

When offering an unorthodox point of view, good authors supply facts, figures, and quotes to buttress their positions, expecting readers to be skeptical of their claims. Knowledgeable authors on the Internet follow these same commonsense guidelines. Be suspicious of authors who expect you to agree with their points of view simply because they've published them on the Internet. In one-on-one encounters, you frequently judge the authority and knowledge of the speaker using criteria you'd be hard pressed to explain. Use your sense of intuition on the Internet, too.

As a researcher (and as a human being), the job of critical thinking requires a combination of healthy skepticism and rabid curiosity. Newsgroups and Web sites tend to focus narrowly on single issues (newsgroups more so than Web sites). Don't expect to find a torrent of opposing views on newsgroup postings; their very nature and reason for existence dampens free-ranging discussions. A newsgroup on *The X-Files* might argue about whether extraterrestrials exist but not whether the program is the premier television show on the air today. Such a discussion would run counter to the purposes of the newsgroup and would be a violation of netiquette. Anyone posting such a message would be flamed, embarrassed, ignored, or otherwise driven away. Your research responsibilities include searching for opposing views by visiting a variety of newsgroups and Web sites. A help here is to fall back on the familiar questions of journalism: who, what, when, where, and why.

part

1

- ▪ **Who** else might speak knowledgeably on this subject? Enter that person's name into a search engine. You might be surprised to find whose work is represented on the Web. (For fun, one of the authors entered the name of a rock-and-roll New York radio disk jockey into MetaCrawler and was amazed to find several pages devoted to the DJ, including sound clips of broadcasts dating back to the sixties, along with a history of his theme song.)

- ▪ **What** event might shed more information on your topic? Is there a group or organization that represents your topic? Do they hold an annual conference? Are synopses of presentations posted on the sponsoring organization's Web site?

- **When** do events happen? Annual meetings or seasonal occurrences can help you isolate newsgroup postings of interest.

- **Where** might you find this information? If you're searching for information on wines, for example, check to see if major wine-producing regions, such as the Napa Valley in California or the Rhine Valley in Germany, sponsor Web sites. These may point you to organizations or information that don't show up in other searches. Remember, Web search engines are fallible; they don't find every site you need.

- **Why** is the information you're searching for important? The answer to this question can lead you to related fields. New drugs, for example, are important not only to victims of diseases but to drug companies and the FDA as well.

part

1

Approach assertions you read from a skeptic's point of view. See if they stand up to critical evaluation or if you're merely emotionally attached to them. Imagine "What if . . . ?" or "What about . . . ?" scenarios that may disprove or at least call into question what you're reading. Try following each assertion you pull from the Internet with the phrase, "On the other hand. . . ." Because you can't leave the sentence hanging, you'll be forced to finish it, and this will help get you into the habit of critically examining information.

These are, of course, the same techniques critical thinkers have employed for centuries, only now you are equipped with more powerful search tools than past researchers may have ever imagined. In the time it took your antecedents to formulate their questions, you can search dozens of potential information sources. You belong to the first generation of college students to enjoy both quantity and quality in its research, along with a wider perspective on issues and the ability to form personal opinions after reasoning from a much wider knowledge base. Certainly, the potential exists for the Internet to grind out a generation of intellectual robots, "thinkers" who don't think but who regurgitate information from many sources. Technology always has its good and bad aspects. However, we also have the potential to become some of the most well-informed thinkers in the history of the world, thinkers who are not only articulate but confident that their opinions have been distilled from a range of views, processed by their own personalities, beliefs, and biases. This is one of the aspects of the Internet that makes this era such an exciting combination of humanism and technology.

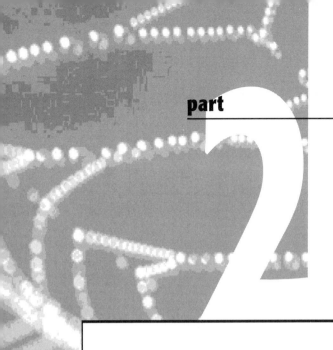

part

Speech Communication Online Activities

In Part I we examined how you relate to other people so that you can discuss ideas for a speech or lurk to gather information about an interest. In this section, we will do online activities to explore some of the ways you can use the Internet.

The Internet has been likened to many different ideas: a fire hose of information (when you only want a sip), a haystack (when you want the needle), and, of course, the most well-known of all, the information superhighway. It's the world's biggest book, with tens of billions of words, but there's no table of contents or index.

You could also think of the Web as the largest library in the world. To enhance your effectiveness, you will need to plan your research strategy. Specifically, we will look at how you can use the resources of the Internet to accomplish four searching strategies:

1. Search the Web to find a speech topic

2. Search the Web to gather supporting evidence

3. Search the Web to use reference sources

4. Search the Web to analyze your audience

Strategy I: Finding a Speech Topic

One of the most difficult steps is finding an appropriate topic for your speech. There are numerous Web based strategies that you can use.

But, first you have to clarify the speaking goal for your presentation. Is your intention to provide information or to persuade your audience? If your goal is persuasive, will you be discussing a timely topic in the news? Or, maybe you will advocate in favor of a legislative solution being debated in the Congress or your community. Another option is to persuade your audience to take a stand on an issue of justice that is being considered by our legal system. Your instructor will provide further thoughts to help you shape a goal for your speech. Consider some of the following as research strategies for finding a topic.

Use a General Topical Browser, Especially for an Informative Speech.

Earlier, you read about how to use AltaVista and Yahoo! to find information on the Web. Now, check out another browsing tool called the Librarians' Index to the Internet. This would be a particularly good starting point for finding informative speech topics.

part
2

1. Start your browser and go to URL **http://sunsite.berkeley.edu/ InternetIndex**.

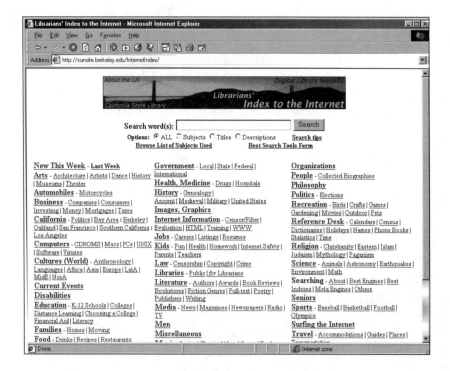

2. Note how the subject page is organized. In the left margin are buttons that allow you go to news stories about topics. In the main part of the page are various subject headings such as Arts, Science, or Health and Medicine.

3. Now select one of the topic areas that appeals to your interests and that you think might be a meaningful, informative topic for your audience.

Find a timely topic that is being discussed in newspapers and current magazines.

The digital newsstand offers many choices, and most newspapers and magazines online allow you to search back issues. Check the section titled "Speech Communication Related Web Sites" later on in this guide to find the URLs for newspapers or magazines that you could use to prepare a speech. Or, go online to the Allyn and Bacon Public Speaking Web site list of periodicals at **http://www.abacon.com/pubspeak/ research/news.html/**.

One of the most useful of these papers is *The Christian Science Monitor* (**http://www.csmonitor.com/**) because of its search capacities and extensive digital files, with reports as far back as 1980. *The New York Times* (**http://www.nytimes.com**) also is especially useful for allowing you to search back issues. Many of the others on the list provide the most recent news. And for topics that are timely, it is useful to use one of them.

There are also a number of magazines on the Internet. As you do research, it is meaningful to recognize that most magazines develop an ideological perspective on current affairs. Read a sample of different views from those on the periodical list.

In addition to browsing individual newspapers, you can also do a global search. One of the most comprehensive guides is the Drudge Report. You can find it at **http://www.drudgereport.com/**.

Note how the Drudge Report is organized in three columns. To the left are search engines for finding headline stories from United Press and the Associated Press. You can also click on any of the newspapers or magazines to go to its current issue. The middle column creates links to opinion pieces by columnists, and the right column is a précis or headline of top stories of the day.

We've explored a variety of ways find an informative speech topic by using search engines, topical lists and news reports. Another method is to use the journalistic method.

part

2

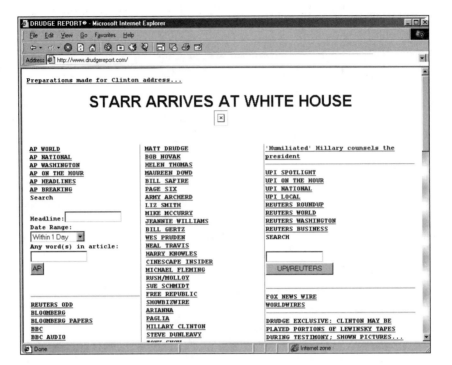

Exercise: 5W's and How for Informative Speeches

Journalists commonly address the questions Who did What? When? Where? Why? and How? The same questions can be starting points for selecting and organizing a topic for an informative speech.

The purpose of this exercise is to use the journalistic method to find a speech topic and to organize a research strategy for finding additional sources on the Internet.

First, point your browser to one of the following URLs:

Who: Use *Biography,* an online magazine at **http://www.biography. com** or consult one of the biographical sources organized by Bob Drucker at **http://www.refdesk.com/factbiog.html.**

What: *Encyberpedia* is an online encyclopedia at **http://www. encyberpedia.com/ency.htm/.** Scroll down to its subject list or use its search functions to find a range of topics. Or go to Drucker's *My Virtual Encyclopedia* at **http://www.refdesk.com/myency.html/.**

When: Search through the American Memory Collection at the Library of Congress at **http://lcweb2.loc.gov/ammem/**.

Where: Take a virtual to tour somewhere with *National Geographic Online* at http://www.nationalgeographic.com/. Or, explore an international topic with *The Web of Culture* at **http://www. worldculture.com/**.

Why: Try the "Why Files," a site funded by the National Science Foundation at **http://whyfiles.news.wisc.edu/**.

How: Learn2.com—the ability utility with explanations on many "how to" topics at **http://www.learn2.com/**.

As you surf for informative topics, make a list of keywords that you can use for using one of the Internet Search Engines. To access search engines, go to **http://www.abacon.com/pubspeak/research/search.html/**.

_____

_____

_____

part

2

Your informative speech ought to have a specific goal. For instance, to **describe** activities at *Mardi Gras,* or to **explain how** contemporary superstitions have historic roots. Phrase three different specific goal statements for an informative speech based on the work you've just done on the Web.

_____

_____

_____

Which specific goal statement is likely to be the best informative topic in light of your interests, the interests and knowledge level of your audience and the research that you have done?

_____

_____

_____

Next rephrase your goal statement as a thesis or topic sentence. The topic sentence is a short declarative sentence that states the central idea of your speech. For instance, if your specific goal was to explain how streaming works in RealAudio transmission of sound files, you might state a topic sentence as "RealAudio transmits sound files as packets of information on the Internet."

_____

_____

_____

Decide which method of organization would work best to develop your topic:

Parts to whole breaks the topic into distinguishable segments.
Chronological sets up a time line.
Spatial organizes points by mapping them geographically.
Causal explains a series of causes and effects.
Process identifies a sequence of steps or stages.

Which method of organization did you choose and why did you select it?

_____

_____

_____

_____

Organize a skeletal outline of your speech with a topic sentence and between three to five main ideas that follow the method of organization you've noted above.

Topic Sentence:

_____

_____

_____

part

2

Main Idea I:

_____

_____

_____

Main Idea II:

_____

_____

_____

Main Idea III:

_____

_____

_____

part

2

There are several other topical browsers for finding informative subjects. You can get to them at **http://www.abacon.com/pubspeak/ assess/topic.html**. There you will also see a special category for subjects in science and technology as well as a whole list of other general topical browsers.

Strategy II: Finding and Evaluating Evidence

In the last section we emphasized surfing the Web to generate ideas for a topic. As effective speakers are thinking about topics for a speech, they are at the same time, finding sources of information. That's what we refer to under Strategy II as finding sources of information and making critical judgements about the value and reliability of evidence. Exercising critical judgement is necessary at any step along the way of speech preparation, and particularly crucial when the goal of your speech is to solve a problem or to persuade members of an audience to take a stand. So, we'll shift our emphasis to sort out some of the ways you can exercise critical thinking to assess evidence.

Check Out Think Tanks for Their Expert Views for Persuasive Speeches

Think tanks undertake extensive research and formulate policy papers on a range of social, political and economic issues. Their findings may be very useful for helping you think about persuasive speeches, especially when your goal is to use a problem-solution approach. There are many different think tanks representing a range of interests and ideological perspectives. One of the most comprehensive is the Electronic Policy Net. A distinctive feature of the Policy Net is its easy-to-navigate image map.

part

2

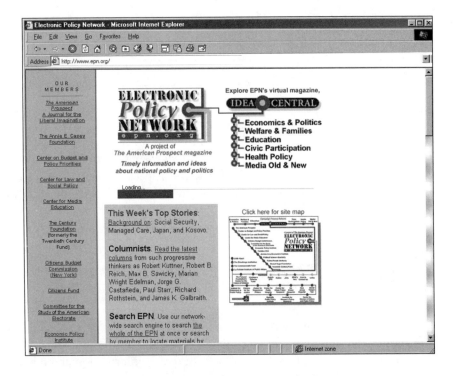

1. Start your browser and go to URL **http://www.epn.org/**.

2. Click on the site map. Follow the red line across the top to find topic areas. Blue lines on the image map are for other think tanks that deal with social and policy organizations.

3. Click on "Health Policy." When you arrive at the page for health related issues, you will see a variety of specific subjects that might be useful as persuasive speech topics.

4. When you click on one of the specific subjects, you will enter a hyper-text analysis of the problem.

It is meaningful to recognize that think tanks are often supported by organizations with an ideological perspective. The Electronic Policy Net, which is sponsored by the *American Prospect,* labels itself as a progressive organization. You can find more think tanks representing a wider political spectrum from the Allyn and Bacon Public Speaking Web site page. Check especially under the link for "Social Problems and Social Policy" at **http://www.abacon.com/pubspeak/assess/topic.html.** You can also search for advocacy groups, including nonprofit organizations, from **http://www.abacon.com/pubspeak/research/groups.html/.**

Testing Evidence

The sheer fact that something is on the Web does not automatically confer credibility on the information. You need to exercise your critical thinking faculties to evaluate the evidence you find. Use the following exercise to consider several standards for judging sources.

part

2

Exercise: Finding and Evaluating Sources of Information on the Web

A recent editorial in *JAMA,* the Journal of the American Medial Association, cautions *Caveant Lector et Viewor*—Let the Reader and Viewer Beware. The authors of that piece, headed by Dr. W. M. Silberg, outline several core standards that we might use to assess information found on the Web.

First, find the *JAMA* guidelines at **http://www.ama-assn.org/sci-pubs/journals/archive/jama/vo l_277/no_15/ed7016x.htm/.**

What are the names of the co-authors of the piece, and what are their qualifications to write on the subject?

_____

_____

_____

_____

_____

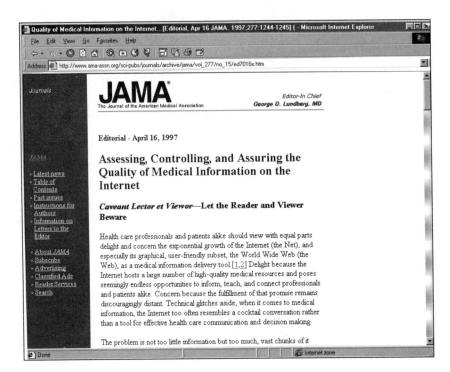

Next, find a source of evidence and assess the quality of the information found at one of the following Web sites (or at a site recommended by your instructor):

National Academy of Sciences: **http://www.nas.edu/**
The Brookings Institution: **http://www.brookings.org/**
Intellectual Capital.com: **http://www.intellectualcapital.com/**
the National Rifle Association: **http://www.nra.org/**
Capitol Hill Blue: **http://www.capitolhillblue.com/**
JAMA: **http://www.ama-assn.org/public/journals/jama/jamahome.htm/**

Assess the information source in light of the *JAMA* standards:

Authorship: Are authors and contributors identified with a citation for their affiliations and relevant credentials?

_____

_____

_____

Attribution: Are references listed for sources that are cited? Is all relevant copyright information included?

_____

_____

_____

Disclosure: Is ownership of the Web site clear? Are sponsors, advertisers, underwriters or sources of commercial funding identified, especially if there might be a conflict of interest?

_____

_____

_____

Currency: Is the page dated to indicate when the content was posted or updated?

_____

_____

_____

What other considerations would you give to this Web page to test the accuracy and reliability of the page?

_____

_____

_____

_____

Take a Stand on a Bill That Has Been Introduced in Congress

Persuasive speeches often advocate that audience members change personal behavior. At other times, your persuasive goal centers on urging a deliberative body to act on an issue. In this next section, we will look at how you can develop a persuasive speech that argues for or against a piece of legislation.

A primary source for such persuasive speeches is the United States Congress. Each year hundreds of bills are introduced on the floor of the

House or the Senate. We will examine how you can locate a bill that re-
lates to one of your interests. You can read background information
about the legislation, and get an update on how far it has progressed
through the legislative chambers. Then take a stand. Urge your classmates to support or reject a piece of legislation by having them contact
their representative or senators. Even if a bill has already been passed,
present a persuasive speech that contends that it is a good bill, or that it
ought to be challenged in the courts! If the bill has not been signed into
law, urge your classmates to write the White House convincing the President to sign or veto the legislation.

We will use THOMAS from the Library of Congress to locate
Congressional information.

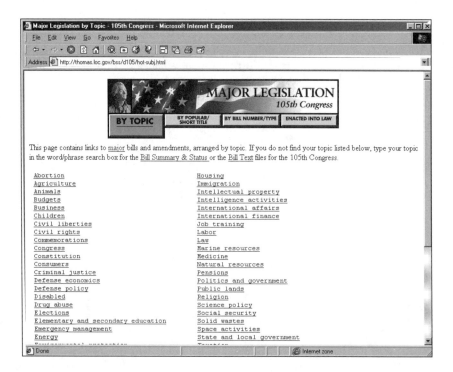

1. Point your browser to **http://thomas.loc.gov/bss/d105/hot-subj.html**.

2. Note the listing of topic areas in alphabetic order. Choose one that
   appeals to you.

3. When you click on a topic, you will go to its page, actually a hypertext page with further links to a wealth of information. The first
   thing to note is the number of the bill. A bill identified as H.R. ###

has been introduced in the House of Representatives. If the bill number is prefaced with S., Thomas has found a Senate bill.

4. Click on a bill number. Click on the "All Bill summary and Status Info" link. This will afford you a number of choices. You can get an update on where the bill is in the legislative process, when it was introduced into its chamber, which committees have or will act on the measure, *Congressional Record* citations on the matter, and even a copy of the bill itself. If you click the link for the text of the bill, you will see additionally how a bill is organized by sections. Many bills are extremely long; so you can look only at those parts that relate most to your speech. The "Digest" version of a bill is a shorter summary.

5. You can also click on the name of the congressional representative or senator who authored the bill. This will help you see other topics that that member of Congress has championed. When you see that a legislator has introduced a number of bills on related issues, you can consider contacting the Web page for that member. There you are likely to find additional resources on a topic that interests you. To Find Web pages for members of the House of Representatives, use **http://www.house.gov/** or for the U.S. Senate **http://www.senate.gov/**.

part
2

6. Check out a page for your congressional representative or one of your senators. About half of the members of the House have pages, and like their fellow Americans, sometimes they have substantive pages with a significant amount of information about issues, and other times they give you little more than shallow political advertising. House pages are found with a link fittingly labeled "Member Pages," and from the Senate click on "Senators." Senate pages are indexed by alphabetic order or by state. For those House members with pages you will find simply an alphabetic listing.

If you don't know the name of your congressional representatives, check out the Project VoteSmart to do a state-by-state or zip code search. VoteSmart is found at **http://www.vote-smart.org/**.

Next, we will use what you've just learned in a concrete situation.

Exercise: Persuasive Speaking on Legislative Topics

The purpose of this activity is to use the World Wide Web to gather information about a topic that is under consideration by lawmakers.

Access the Internet address **http://thomas.loc.gov.** (An alternative source to use for this exercise is Project VoteSmart's Congress Track. You can find it at **http://www.vote-smart.org/congresstrack/.**)

Click on the button for "Major Legislation by Topic" and choose one of the topic areas in the alphabetic list.

What interests you personally about the topic area?

_____

_____

_____

What is the bill number and the title for a piece of legislation in this area? Next, who is the sponsor for that bill?

_____

_____

_____

part

2

Now click on the bill number. Assess the stated goal of the legislation. Do you agree or disagree with that goal?

Click on "All Bill Summary and Status Information" to see if floor action has been taken on the measure. Then, find a speech or debate from the *Congressional Record* on this matter. (Look for the notation "CR" for the *Congressional Record*. Did any of the remarks or debates on the floor provide good reasons for supporting or advocating against the law?

_____

_____

_____

Determine the current status of the bill. Based on how far the bill has gotten, what will be your persuasive goal?

■ to urge members of the House or Senate to support the bill?

■ to urge the President to sign or veto the bill?

■ (if floor action has not been taken) to urge members of Congress to act on the legislation, perhaps to reintroduce a re-worked version of the bill?

State your specific goal as a topic sentence.

_____

_____

_____

Make a list of pertinent email addresses and Web page URLs for congressional representatives, senators, House or Senate committees, or for the White House. You may also use **http://www.house.gov/, http://www. senate.gov/,** or **http://www.whitehouse.gov/** for this part of the exercise.

_____

_____

_____

Next, find a federal agency that may have bearing on this topic. Federal agencies often provide input to Congressional deliberations. They perform their main function of executing and enforcing most Congressional legislation. You can find federal agencies at the Federal Web Locator. Use **http://www.law.vill.edu/fed-agency/.**

part

2

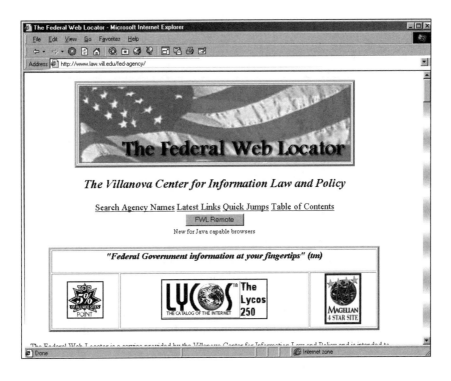

What are pertinent Web addresses for an agency or bureau that deals with this topic? What kinds of information are available that would be pertinent to your topic?

_____

_____

_____

_____

_____

_____

Finally, use the Internet Law Library for the House of Representatives to find other federal or state laws that are pertinent to your topic. The URL for the law library is **http://law.house.gov/90.htm/**. What did you find that provides leads for further research?

part

2

_____

_____

_____

_____

_____

_____

There are additional resources for doing topics on legislation at the Allyn and Bacon Public Speaking Web Site. In particular, go to **http://www.abacon.com/pubspeak/research/gov.html**. From this page, you will also be able to link to federal agencies, the White House, and to your state and local government agencies.

Speak About a Pending or Contentious Court Case

You can also choose a persuasive speech topic that deals with a legal question. Legal questions are often very intricate and complex. One way to learn about the workings of the justice system is to see how legal lobbying groups approach an issue. Keep in mind that the main purpose of a lobby is to advocate a position. So, you can decide whether you agree with their position or not. At the same time, effective lobbying groups responsibly inform the public. To illustrate this, we will use the Web site for the American Civil Liberties Union (ACLU).

Exercise: Do You Agree with the ACLU?

The goal of this exercise is to explore some of the resources on the ACLU home page and to exercise critical judgment for developing a persuasive speech on an issue of Free Speech.

First, go to the ACLU Web site at **http://www.aclu.org/**. Note that the ACLU page uses an image map. Earlier, we discussed the image map as a navigation tool. As you run your mouse down the topics listed in the right hand column of the page, you will see your cursor become a finger pointer. Click the "Free Speech" option.

Click on the "Index of ACLU Free Speech Materials" to choose one of the ACLU Briefing Papers. After you've read the paper, consider the following questions:

What aspect of free speech do you think is most important?

Why? _____

_____

_____

_____

Do you agree or disagree with the general principles about free speech that the ACLU advocates?

_____

_____

_____

_____

_____

_____

_____

_____

part

2

Note some of the court cases that the ACLU cites in its briefing:

_____

_____

_____

_____

_____

State a persuasive goal for a speech about free speech:

_____

_____

_____

part

2

Next, use a page from the American Communication Association (ACA) Center for Communication Law. Go to its this page at **http://www.americancomm.org/~aca/american.htm.**

List at least three URLs that you found from this page that are pertinent to your topic.

_____

_____

_____

To find the best sources of information about legal questions we turn to primary documents written by officials in the judicial system. Explore at least one of the following to find three more primary sources:

- FindLaw **<http://www.findlaw.com/>**   This source allows you to search for syllabi of cases before the U.S. Supreme Court (the syllabus is a brief synopsis of the case), or to find topics at any of the appellate courts.
- Federal Court Locator **<http://www.law.vill.edu/Fed-Ct/fedcourt.html/>** It does the same kind of searches as FindLaw.

_____

_____

_____

_____

_____

_____

Strategy III: Using Reference Sources: Encyclopedias, Dictionaries, Glossaries, and Thesauri

How many reference books can you keep on your desk at one time? Most of us would run out of room if we tried to keep as many reference books at arm's length on our desk as can be accessed by letting our fingers do the reaching on a keyboard—one that is "keywording" search commands on the Web, that is. When you use the Web you've got just about any reference source you'll need. To explore that idea, turn to the next exercise, called "Look It Up."

part

2

Exercise: Look It Up

The purpose of this exercise is to explore reference sources on the Web, looking up words and expressions that you can use in crafting your speech. The goal of this exercise is to try a variety of types of dictionaries and glossaries and writing tools that are available on the Web.

First, point your browser to a compendium of reference sources at **http://www.abacon.com/pubspeak/organize/dict.html**. Notice the range of types of sources for finding general and specific vocabulary terms, literary sources, scientific and technical, legal definitions, and the special parlance of the Internet. Bookmark that page, and then look up the items in bold print that are listed below. Along with the definition that you find, write down the URL for the Web source that you used for the term.

1. Employees of the United States Government speak their own short hand language to label various federal agencies. What is meant by the term *SBA*?

_____

_____

What source did you use? _____

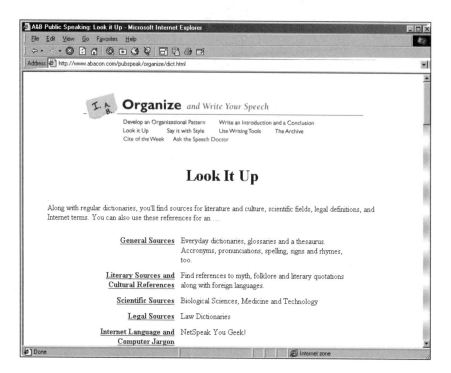

2. Reading a book of folk tales, you came across the name Cormoran. Who is that?

_____

_____

What source did you use? _____

3. Did Shakespeare have the same meaning for the word _sometimes_ as we do today?

_____

_____

What source did you use? _____

4. How many different meanings can you come up for the word _line_ and other terms related to it, such as _linear, lining, underline,_ and so on?

_____

_____

What source did you use? _____

5. Who was the mythological character Pegasus?

_____

_____

What source did you use? _____

6. What does a legal contract mean if people hold property under the status of _tenancy in common_?

_____

_____

What source did you use? _____

7. In your multimedia class, what is the meaning of the term interlaced GIF? And how do you pronounce GIF? Does the first letter sound more like the first consonant in _gift_ or _jump_?

_____

_____

What source did you use? _____

part 2

8. What is the meaning of the medical term _glioblastoma_?

_____

_____

What source did you use? _____

9. How is the use of evidence governed in a court of law in light of the exclusionary rule?

_____

_____

What source did you use? _____

10. What is a homophone for the word _sun_? And for that matter, what is a homophone?

_____

_____

What source did you use? _____

11. On a bulletin board someone posted a message with the expression ROTFL and then used the expression ;-). What do these interjections mean?

   _____

   _____

   What source did you use? _____

12. What is the meaning of the Latin phrase *saepius sepius*?

   _____

   _____

   What source did you use? _____

13. If someone is employed as a *jawbone breaker,* what kind of work does that person do?

   _____

   _____

   What source did you use? _____

14. What do computer nerds mean when they speak of a MIDI file?

   _____

   _____

   What source did you use? _____

part

2

Strategy IV: Analyzing Your Audience

In your public speaking class, you've no doubt discussed how important it is to adapt your speech to the audience. And, you've probably made some good observations of the members of your class. You can also do research on the Web to analyze your audience. In the next exercise, we will find data to help you assess your listeners. We will look at demographic, psychographic, and ideological methods of analysis.

Exercise: Draw a Demographic and Psychographic Profile

Public speakers attempt to adapt to their listeners after assessing the demographic background of the audience. Factors such as the age, sex, race and ethnicity, income level, educational level, religion and philosophical orientations, professional background, and family makeup and sexual orientation are demographic groupings that characterize an audience.

The purpose of this exercise is to work with data available from the U.S. Census Bureau at its Web site. In doing this activity, suppose that you have been asked to present a speech to a group in the community in which you reside. Suppose further that the makeup of your audience is representative of the community as a whole. For purposes of this exercise, we will define your community as everyone who lives within the zip code where you live, or where your college is located.

First, use data from the U.S. Census Bureau. A handy online reference source for demographic data is its Census Gazetteer. You can find data for your zip code or for the county in which you live. That address is **http://www.census.gov/cgi-bin/gazetteer**.

part

2

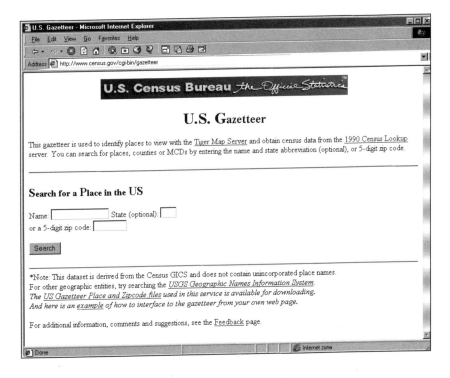

Choose some of the demographic fields. Then draw a pie chart in the circle below to represent one of the following demographics for your target audience:

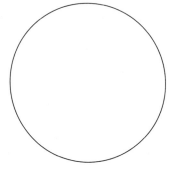

■ percentages by age
■ percentages by sex
■ percentages by race
  and ethnic background

To what degree do you think the percentages of that demographic on your pie chart is representative of the class group?

Next, draw another pie chart that is more representative of your class:

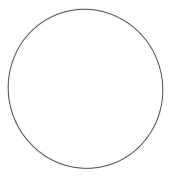

Do you think that the demographic distribution of your class affects the way you tailor your speech? How?

_____

_____

_____

What other demographic factors are important for your class audience?

_____

_____

_____

Effective speakers also adapt on the basis of psychographic factors. Psychographic dimensions of the audience include the value system, lifestyle, and ideology that each class member operates from.

For the next part of the exercise, we will once again use a zip code. We will go to the Web page for Equifax, which is a marketing research firm that develops psychological profiles of neighborhoods. First, go to the URL **http://www.natdecsys.com/lifequiz.html/**, and simply type in your zip code.

Lifestyle profiles are also based on attitude surveys, demographic categories, geographic factors and consumer habits.

What lifestyle descriptions are identified for your community?

_____

_____

_____

Do you think this profile fits your community? If yes, how? If no, what other label would you use?

_____

_____

_____

part

2

Is your class representative of the broader zip code community that you used? If yes, how would you appeal to the class in light of the lifestyle profile? If no, how would you develop a different approach to your class as an audience than to the community as a whole?

_____

_____

_____

_____

Analyzing Political Ideologies

A political ideology is a conceptual framework that an individual uses to analyze issues. We act on our ideology in the choices we make to identify with others politically, and the positions we articulate. Our political ideology is reflected in the attitudes that we hold about the proper role of government.

The next goal of this exercise is to identify one's own political ideology and to analyze the audience for your speech in light of its ideology. We will also look at some of the Web pages of political organizations for discussion of the underlying political ideology that these organizations represent.

First, find and take the "World's Smallest Political Quiz." Go to **http://www.self-gov.org/quiz.html/**.

Based on the political quiz, what is your political ideology? Do you agree with that characterization? If you don't agree with that designation, what label would you use to describe your political ideology?

_____

_____

_____

What political and social views that you hold are consistent with your political ideology?

_____

_____

_____

Based on your observations of your class and from hearing speeches from other class members, do you feel that most members of your class audience share your views?

_____

_____

_____

As you adapt your next speech to your audience, what aspects of a shared ideology can you emphasize? How will you adapt to segments of your class audience that hold an ideology different from yours?

_____

_____

_____

The "World's Smallest Political Quiz" was created by Paul Schmidt and sponsored by an organization called "Advocates for Self Government." Go to Paul Schmidt's home page at **http://world.std.com/~pschmidt/**. What is his political ideology?

_____

_____

_____

Analyze the political ideology that is reflected in one of the following Web pages.

Children's Defense Fund: **http://www.childrensdefense.org/**

Citizens for an Alternative Tax System: **http://www.cats.org/**

The Concord Coalition: **http://www.concordcoalition.org/**

Democratic National Committee: **http://www.democrats.org/**

Democratic Socialists of America: **http://www.dsausa.org/**

Green Parties of North American: **http://www.greens.org/**

Natural Law Party: **http://www.natural-law.org/**

Reform Party: **http://www.reformparty.org/**

Republican National Committee: **http://www.rnc.org/**

part

2

What is an ideologically based position held by this organization that would make an effective persuasive speech in light of your own ideology and your audience's?

_____

_____

_____

Speech Communication Related Web Sites

 General Search Engines

AltaVista

http://www.altavista.digital.com/

One of the most powerful keyword search engines because it searches for Web pages or Usenet groups.

AOL NetFind

http://www.aol.com/netfind/

Use keyword searching or check one of the time saver areas.

Electric Library

http://www.elibrary.com/

You can use this commercial metasearch tool for finding a host of sources. There is a monthly fee to use it, however. The library also offers a thirty-day free trial.

Excite

http://www.excite.com/

Excite will perform concept or keyword searches using a natural language approach. You can further tailor a search to find sites that have been reviewed by topical areas, called Channels.

Galaxy

http://www.einet.net/cgi-bin/wais-text-multi?/

Galaxy is one of the most comprehensive Internet search engines because you can tell it to search for gopher and telnet sites as well as pages on

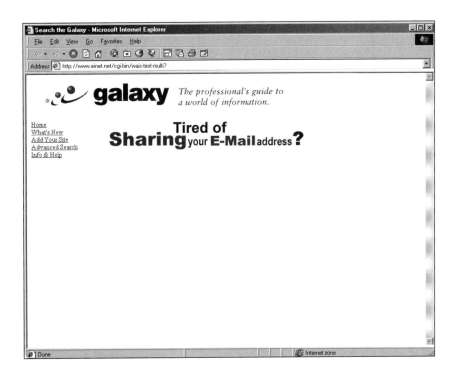

the Web. You can also narrow the search by identifying whether you want Galaxy to find pages for any of your particular search terms or all of them.

Hotbot

`http://www.hotbot.com/`

This search tool is sponsored by HotWired Magazine. It can do rather impressive searches for multimedia files. It also has built in chat capabilities if you have a JAVA based browser.

Infoseek

`http://www.infoseek.com/`

Along with keyword searching functions found on most other search engines, Infoseek features Quickseek, so that you can customize searching functions on your desktop. MSIE users can also download an ActiveX control that works with 3.02 browser (or higher) to integrate infoseek search capabilties into your browser toolbar.

Internet Sleuth

http://www.isleuth.com/

The Internet Sleuth is a metasearch engine that searches through the databases of as many as six searching sites at one time. You can also use it to browse or to do keyword searching for rated sites, business sites, discussion groups or software.

Lycos

http://www.lycos.com/

Lycos enables you to search for sound and picture files. Another fun feature is its mapping function. You can locate your street address on a city map of your community.

Snap.com

http://www.snap.com/

This engine allows the user to personalize their news and weather and search through pre-categorized link selections.

Webcrawler

http://www.webcrawler.com/

Developed for America Online, but you don't have to be an AOL subscriber to use it. Check out its statistics about the most commonly accessed URLs on the Net.

Topical Browsers

Argus Clearinghouse

http://www.clearinghouse.net/

The clearinghouse is a virtual library organized by what it calls "topical guides." These are lists developed by "Cybrarians" who have investigated particular subjects.

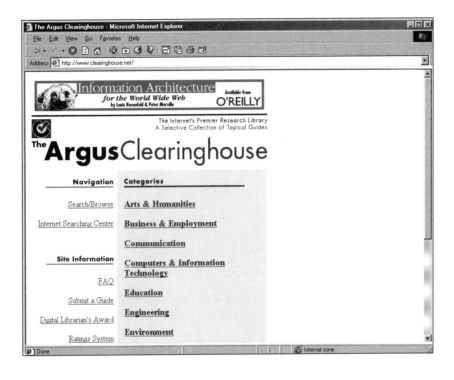

part
2

World Wide Web Virtual Library

`http://www.w3.org/hypertext/DataSources/bySubject/`
`Overview.html/`

Affiliated with CERN, this virtual library is organized by an extensive list of subject areas.

Yahoo!

`http://www.yahoo.com/`

One of the best for browsing topical lists of types of sites. It is the most extensively used search engine on the Web. Its main directories are Computers and Internet, Education, Entertainment, Government, Health, Recreation, Reference, Regional, Science, Social Science, and Society and Culture. Each of these branches to more topical subdirectories to browse.

Other Searching Tools

Find Internet Directories:

AcqWeb's Directory of Publishers and Vendors

http://www.library.vanderbilt.edu/law/acqs/pubr.html

Contains directories of email addresses, and Web and Gopher sites, as well as listings by subject.

Who-Where Yellow Pages

http://www.whowhere.com/business.html

Finds email addresses, personal Web pages and regular phone numbers.

Find Advocacy Groups:

The Mining Co.

http://www.miningco.com/

Reviewers have selected the best sites in over 600 categories making this location a great place to start in any type of searching on the Internet.

Think Tanks

http://a2z.lycos.com/Government/Politics/
Institutes_and_Think_Tanks/

Browse an alphabetic list of policy study organizations that was developed by Lycos.

Find Books and Libraries:

Bibliomania

http://www.mk.net/~dt/Bibliomania/

This site from the UK provides online versions of classic works of fiction and non-fiction. There is also a section for poetry and reference works.

Some of the titles are in PDF format and require the Adobe Acrobat Reader.

Books Online

`http://www.cs.cmu.edu/Web/bookauthors.html`

Scroll down the alphabetic list of authors. Good for finding classics that have been digitized.

Library of Congress

`http://lcweb.loc.gov/homepage/lchp.html`

Go to the national library. You can find information about exhibits at the Library, as well as its holdings.

Libweb

`http://sunsite.berkeley.edu/Libweb?`

From Berkeley, this server provides links to hundreds of library collections around the world.

Find Reference Sources:

part

2

The Librarians' Index to the Internet

`http://sunsite.berkeley.edu/InternetIndex/`

Enter a keyword or narrow your search to one of more than thirty categories to find the reference information you need.

Find Newspaper or Magazine Stories:

The Drudge Report

`http://www.drudgereport.com/`

Updated daily by Matt Drudge, this list links you to headline stories and a wide variety of newspaper and wire service sources. A special feature is the set of links to syndicated columnists.

E & P Media INFO

`http://www.mediainfo.com/emediajs/media-types.`
`htm?category=newspaper/`

Using Editor and Publisher Media INFO, you can find online versions of newspapers from around the world.

News Directory.com

`http://www.newsdirectory.com/`

News Directory.com has created a collection of links to worldwide media sources, including newspapers, magazines, journals, TV stations and more.

Pathfinder

`http://www.pathfinder.com/`

The Pathfinder page will help you find online editions of the various magazines that are part of the Time-Warner Network.

Total News

`http://www.totalnews.com/`

A one-stop cite for finding various media outlets, including FOX News, MSNBC, CNN Interactive, CBS News, USA Today, ABC Radio, NPR, Reuters, the Nando Times, and TIME Daily. With its Paradigm News feature you can type in keywords for headline news to locate stories from various news sources.

Find Electronic "E-zines":

Electronic Journals in the World Wide Web Virtual Library

`http://www.edoc.com/ejournal/`

The e-journal page is organized by topic. Of special interest are student-refereed journals as well as peer-reviewed titles.

E-Zines Database Menu

`http://www.dominis.com/Zines/`

Identifies many e-zines on a broad range of topics.

Nerdworld Media

`http://www.nerdworld.com/users/dstein/nw30.html`

This site provides an extensive list and links to online magazines.

Find Usenet Discussion Groups:

DejaNews

`http://www.dejanews.com/`

This is one of the more user-friendly ways to take part in newsgroups. It uses your Web browser to emulate a newsreader.

Liszt of Newsgroups

`http://liszt.bluemarble.net/news/`

This is a user-friendly directory to browse or search for a newsgroup. The opening page enables you to do a keyword search of usenet newsgroups. To find online discussion groups, check the LISTS button for

part

2

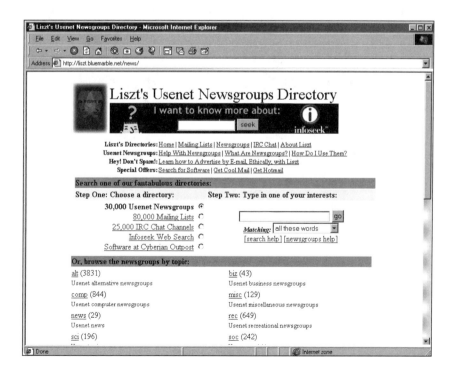

another page where you can find listserv, listproc, and majordomo groups. If you want to browse, try the Liszt Select option.

Tile.Net/News

`http://tile.net/news/`

This source uses alphabetic lists that you can browse to find newsgroup topics.

RemarQ

`http://www.remarq.com`

RemarQ provides Usenet services to both individuals and ISP's. This site allows for quick access to category-specific Usenet groups.

Usenet: FAQs

part
2

`http://www.cis.ohio-state.edu/hypertext/faq/usenet/FAQ-List.html/`

A FAQ is a list of frequently asked questions about a newsgroup and how to participate in it. It is often useful to find the FAQ before subscribing.

Find E-Mail Discussion Groups:

Communication Institute for Online Scholarship

`http://www.cios.org/`

This organization sponsors "hotlines," email discussion groups that share information about communication scholarship. You can also join one of their forums. An individual or institutional membership is required for access.

Liszt Directory of Email Discussion Groups

`http://www.liszt.com/`

This URL will take you directly to the LIST of discussion groups.

Email Discussion and Newsgroups for Scholars

`http://n2h2.com/KOVACS/`

This list is a searchable directory to find scholarly sources for numerous academic disciplines.

Find Online Bulletin Boards:

Forum One

`http://www.forumone.com/`

Search this index of 200,000 different online groups.

Find Live Events and Chat

Netguide

`http://www.netguide.com/`

Find out when live events and chats take place dealing with stories in the news, shopping, health, the Internet, money, travel, entertainment, life and sports.

Timecast

`http://www.timecast.com/`

Daily guide to RealAudio and RealVideo programming in news, entertainment and sports. In addition, there is a calendar of events for the entire upcoming month.

part

2

Yahoo! Chat Events

`http://events.yahoo.com/`

Use this topical list of choices for a variety of types of online interaction. You can also find out times for live chat on the Yahoo! Politics page: http://events.yahoo.com/Government/Politics/.

Find Government Sources:

FEDSTATS

`http://www.fedstats.gov/`

This site is maintained by the Federal Interagency Council on Statistical Policy. You can find statistics from over 70 federal agencies.

FedWorld Information Network

`http://www.fedworld.gov/`

part

2

Developed by NTIS (National Technology Information System) this is an excellent source for finding a host of government sources.

National Archives and Records Administration

`http://www.nara.gov/`

"NARA's mission is to ensure ready access to essential evidence that documents the rights of American citizens, the actions of federal officials, and the national experience."

Government Xchange

`http://www.info.gov/`

This page provides access to government documents.

Govbot

`http://cobar.cs.umass.edu/ciirdemo/Govbot/`

This robot from the Center for Intelligent Information Retrieval will search through the databases for government agencies and military sites around the country.

National Technical Information Service

http://www.ntis.gov/

This agency from the Commerce Department can help you search for government reports.

Project VoteSmart

http://www.vote-smart.org/

Explore this page for the types of information that you can learn about your congressional representative or senators.

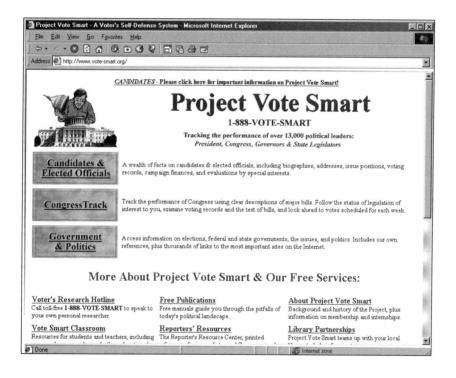

part

2

THOMAS, Legislative Information on the Internet

http://thomas.loc.gov/

Library of Congress site for learning about Congress and government. You can research current legislation and the *Congressional Record* since 1993. To go directly to the *Congressional Record* use http://lcweb.loc. gov/global/legislative/congrec.html/.

U.S. Government Printing Office

`http://www.gpo.gov/`

The GPO is an arm of the Congress, and it is the largest publisher in the world. This site allows you to access its catalog. It does not link you to the sources themselves, however.

U.S. National Library of Medicine

`http://www.nlm.nih.gov/`

Use this for free medline searches and for finding reliable information on health related topics.

World-Wide Web Virtual Library of U.S. Government Information Sources:

`http://www.nttc.edu/gov_res.html/`

This site is maintained by the National Technology Transfer Center. It links you to numerous federal agencies and government commissions.

Find State and Local Government Agencies

State and Local Governments on the Net

`http://www.piperinfo.com/state/states.html`

Search this site maintained by Piper Resources to find servers for each of the fifty states. On each page, you will also find links to various branches of the state government, agencies, and county or city servers on the Internet.

Dogpile.com

`http://www.dogpile.com/`

"Dogpile.com is a useful searching tool that allows the user to search from 20 different search engines at once. The user can also get stock quotes, weather forecasts, yellow and white pages and maps at dogpile.com."

Find Legal and Judicial Sources:

The E-Mail Address Book

`http://www.emailbook.com/`

The Internet Directory of E-mail addresses has a search engine for people's e-mail addresses. To start a search the user types in the person's first and last name.

FindLaw

```
http://www.findlaw.com/
```

Do topical search with a broad range of types of issues and court decisions.

LawRunner

```
http://www.lawrunner.com/
```

LawRunner works in conjunction with AltaVista to target legal resources in the AltaVista database. You can also use it to narrow your search to U.S. government agencies, particular jurisdictions or to a state.

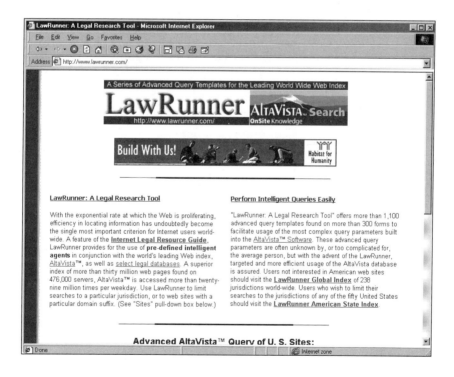

part

2

USSC+

```
http://www.usscplus.com/
```

U.S. Supreme Court Database. This is a very comprehensive source providing decisions for cases from 1967–95.

U.S. Department of Justice Search

http://www.usdoj.gov/

Use this page to find crime statistics and legal matters.

Find Multimedia Materials and Browser Plug-ins:

Images and Graphics from the Librarians' Index to the Internet

http://sunsite.berkeley.edu/cgi-bin/searchindex?title
=Images,+Graphics&query=images+graphics&searchtype
=subjects

This site provides links to 28 databases for finding clip art and images.

Lycos Pictures and Sounds

http://www.lycos.com/lycosmedia.html/

Try out this function of lycos to locate images and sound files that it has indexed.

NetGuide Plug-in Primer

http://www.netguide.com/special/primers/plugins/
home.html/

This is a handy reference source about plug-ins with instructions for where and how to download them.

Stroud's Consummate Internet Apps List

http://cws.iworld.com/

Search through its list of 16 and 32 bit shareware options to find software for your multimedia computer.

World Wide Web Virtual Library for Audio

http://www.comlab.ox.ac.uk/archive/audio.html

This WWW3 library provides links to live radio programming around the world. This site also has some useful links for finding sound archives, Usenet groups dealing with audio, and locating software for

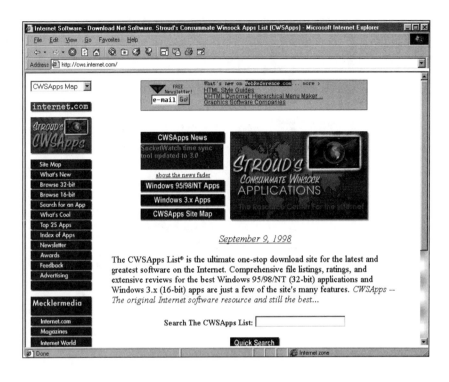

sound. Listen to it all: from bird songs at the Australian Botanical Gardens to tunes from the Rock 'n' Roll Hall of Fame.

Advocacy Groups

The ACLU

http://www.aclu.org/

On most contemporary hot button legal issues, the American Civil Liberties Union has taken a stand that might start you out with choosing a legal topic. The page also provides briefs submitted by the ACLU in high profile court cases.

The Brookings Institution

http://www.brookings.org/

This is a very good source for topics if you are interested in domestic policy, especially economic issues. Be sure to click on its areas for policy briefs.

part

2

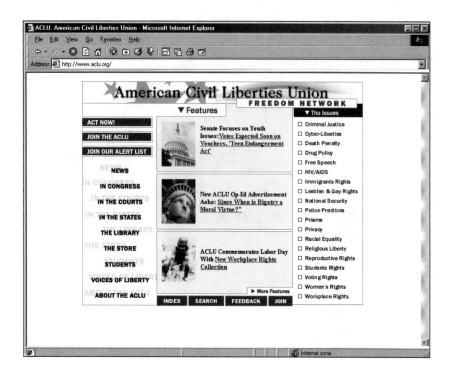

The Cato Institute

http://www.cato.org/

This is a conservative think tank that has published studies on a variety of domestic and international policy areas. The Cato Institute also offers an option to do a keyword search for topic ideas. Note the archive of RealAudio and RealVideo presentations on policy questions.

The Electronic Policy Network

http://www.epn.org/

This page is sponsored by The American Prospect, a progressive political magazine. The links from this page lead to studies on a host of domestic policy issues.

Policy.com—The Policy News and Information Service

`http://www.policy.com/community/advoc.html`

This site offers the user many links to sites concerning advocacy groups. Listed in alphabetical order, these links range from 20/20 Vision, an environmental group, to Zero Population Group, a grass roots group focusing on the population crisis.

Rand Corporation

`http://www.rand.org/`

Highlight its "HOT TOPICS," "Research Areas," and "Publications" for policy studies, especially on issues of national defense and international affairs.

National Academy of Sciences

`http://www.nas.edu/`

This site provides an alphabetic list of current social problems studied from a scientific perspective.

National Academy of Sciences Behavior and Social Sciences

`http://www4.nas.edu/WWWCAT.`
`NSF/6db31770b80499f4852564e400608650?OpenView`

The NAS also has a link to societal issues studied by a variety of social sciences on this page. Be sure to scroll down to the online reports for links on pertinent to your informative or persuasive speech.

Townhall.com

`http://www.townhall.com/`

Enter the townhall where you can find a number of organizations that develop a conservative point of view.

part

2

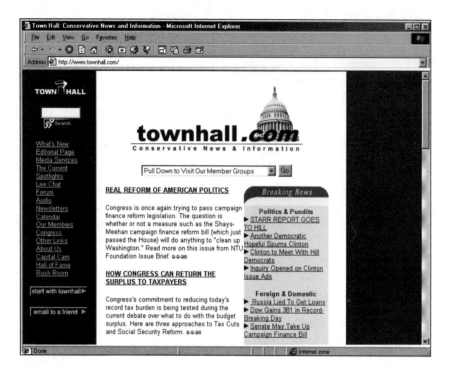

Encyclopedias and Reference Sources

Encyclopedias:

Encyclopedia.com

`http://www.encyclopedia.com/`

This online encyclopedia allows the user to search for a term/phrase or browse by letter.

Encyclopedia Britannica

`http://www.ebig.com/index.html/`

This page provides information about the online version of the *Encyclopedia Britannica*. To access it you will need to be a subscriber.

Let's Find Out

`http://www.letsfindout.com/`

The Knowledge Adventure Encyclopedia is a great homework helper. Users can search for terms to be researched or browse by subject. There are lots of subjects here, perfect for a school project.

Index Encyberpedia

`http://www.encyberpedia.com/ency.htm`

This completely online encyclopedia provides coverage of a broad range of subjects.

The Encyclopedia Mythica

`http://www.pantheon.org/mythica/`

This collection of links about myth, legends and folklore includes hypertext for some of its entries.

Dictionaries and Glossaries:

part

2

The Acronym Finder

`http://www.mtnds.com/af/`

Type in an acronym and this site will search its collection of 75,000 to find a match.

Animated American Sign Language Dictionary

`http://www.bconnex.net/~randys/`

See and understand sign communications.

Brewer's Dictionary of Phrase and Fable

`http://www.mk.net/~dt/Bibliomania/Reference/`
`PhraseAndFable/`

Popular in hardcover since 1879, there is now a hypertext version. Use the alphabetic method of browsing or go to the main Bibliomania page to search at http://www.bibliomania.com.

The CMU Pronouncing Dictionary

http://www.speech.cs.cmu.edu/cgi-bin/cmudict/

Developed at Carnegie Mellon, this is a pronouncing dictionary that uses a system of phonetic markings.

The Ruth H. Hooker Research Library and Technical Information Center

http://infoweb.nrl.navy.mil/catalogs_and_databases/Writing.html

A collection of sites for all writing needs. Users will find links to dictionaries, Bartlett's quotations, encyclopedias and more.

English Oxford Dictionary Online

http://www.oed.com/

This is the online version of the *Oxford English Dictionary Online*.

On-line Dictionaries

http://www.facstaff.bucknell.edu/rbeard/diction.html

A very large resource of dictionaries, thesauri and other writing tools. This site is equipped with a search engine and the user can choose between a number of languages for the dictionary.

Latin–English Dictionary

http://humanum.arts.cuhk.edu.hk/Lexis/Latin/

Find those expressions in italic that make their way into English sentences here. Especially useful for law, medicine, or gardening. Declaro!

Life Science Dictionary

http://biotech.chem.indiana.edu/search/dict-search.html/

Developed by BioTech, you can use this to define terms in various fields of biology, chemistry, ecology, medicine, pharmacology, and toxicology.

Biotechnology Dictionary

`http://biotech.icmb.utexas.edu/pages/dictionary.html`

This is a life science dictionary. It allows the user to search biotechnical terms, term fragments, and definitions to get back the actual term.

OneLook Dictionaries

`http://www.onelook.com/`

This dictionary includes categories in computers, technology, business, science, medicine, religion, sports and just about anything else.

A Dictionary of Scientific Quotations

`http://naturalscience.com/dsqhome.html/`

Quotes from famous scientists in the natural sciences, social sciences, environmental studies, and technology.

A Semantic Rhyming Dictionary

`http://www.cs.cmu.edu/~dougb/rhyme.html`

Type in a search word and you can see if there is a perfect match, a syllable rhyme or a homophone. Sounds like?

A Shakespearian Glossary

`http://eserver.org/langs/shakespeare-glossary.txt/`

Stuck on a phrase attributed to the bard, find it here in this alphabetic listing of words from Shakespeare—for sooth!

The Unofficial Smiley Dictionary

`http://www.eff.org/papers/eegtti/eeg_286.html`

Check out those strange typographical symbols inserted in email messages. ;-)

Usenet Acronym Dictionary

`http://homepages.ihug.co.nz/~tajwileb/dictionary.html`

These are the forms of verbal shorthand commonly used on bulletin boards and Usenet discussions . . . BRB!

part
2

WWWebster Dictionary:

http://www.m-w.com/netdict.htm

This is the online version of the Merriam Webster dictionary. You can search for phrases as well as words.

The WorldWideWeb Acronym and Abbreviation Server

http://www.ucc.ie/info/net/acronyms/

In addition to finding the meaning of an acronym, this database allows you to type in words to determine if they are included in an acronym.

What is

http://whatis.com/.

Handy reference for speaking the language of computer geeks. You can scroll through a top frame of alphabetic terms or search using Excite.

part

2

Writing Tools

Bartlett's Familiar Quotations:

http://www.cc.columbia.edu/acis/bartleby/bartlett/

Need a quote for your speech? Get it online from this classic source.

Garbl's Writing Resources On Line

http://pw1.netcom.com/~garbl1/writing.html

This site has many links to help the user write the perfect paper. These links are split into: English grammar, style, usage, plain language, words, reference sources, on-line writing experts, word play and books on writing.

Writing References from Ohio State

http://osunlabs.newark.ohio-state.edu/writing-lab/ref.htm

The Ohio State Writing Lab presents useful tools for any type of composition, in any type of discipline. These references include: *Webster's Dic-*

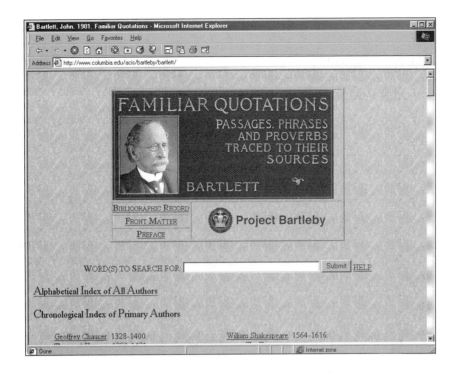

tionary, Oxford English Dictionary, Rôget's Thesaurus, and 130 Grammar Handouts compiled by Purdue University.

The Purdue University Writing Lab

http://owl.english.purdue.edu/

Useful source for writing tools.

Rôget's Thesaurus

http://humanities.uchicago.edu/forms_unrest/
ROGET.html/

This is the 1911 edition, but still useful to find the synonym you need.

Strunk & White: The Elements of Style

http://www.columbia.edu/acis/bartleby/strunk/

Got a grammatical question or concern about written form? You can find the answer here.

Newspapers

The Chicago Tribune

http://www.chicago.tribune.com/

This is the interactive edition for news from Chicago.

The Christian Science e-Monitor

http://www.csmonitor.com/

From the Site Express navigation tools, you can explore the wealth of features on the e-Monitor including RealAudio reports from Monitor Radio called Audio Briefs and an excellent forum. The Monitor also enables you to search its archive for issues as far back as 1980.

The Los Angeles Times

http://www.latimes.com/

News from the West coast. A fee based archive of past stories is also available.

The New York Times

`http://www.nytimes.com/`

Premier national newspaper; "all the news that's fit to print" online.

Philadelphia Online

`http://www.phillynews.com/`

You can select online versions of the Philadelphia Inquirer or the Philadelphia Daily News.

Real Cities

`http://www.realcities.com/thesites/index.htm/`

Links to 31 Knight Ridder newspapers around the country. Use the image map to pick a region of the country or scroll to browse the list of newspapers.

part

2

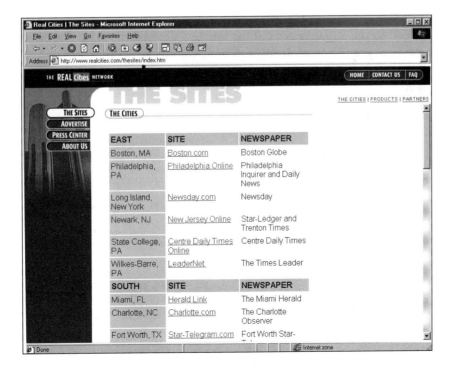

USA Today

http://www.usatoday.com/

Daily national newspaper, and like its print counterpart, the online version is heavy on graphics and color, and light on the news.

Village Voice Worldwide

http://www.villagevoice.com/

Published weekly, this online version has the same social commentary and pop culture features as the tabloid version. Want to rent an apartment in SOHO?

Wall Street Journal

http://public.wsj.com/

This online version requires a subscription. You may do a two-week free trial subscription.

The Washington Post

http://www.washingtonpost.com/

Read the online version of the premier Washington daily. The online Post allows you to jump to sections with its keyword search.

Wire Services

The Associated Press

http://www.newsday.com/ap/national.htm/

This link from newsday.com allows you to access the Associated Press.

KnightRidder—Information for Life

http://www.knightridder.com/

Knight Ridder Newservice provides the user with press releases, financial news, job opportunities, and some information about the company.

part
2

Online Magazines

Atlantic Monthly

http://www.theatlantic.com/atlantic/

The online version is called Atlantic Unbound and provides you with complete texts and an interactive forum called "Post and Riposte."

CNN/TIME Magazine's Allpolitics

http://www.allpolitics.com/

Get the day's summary of news. To join the discussion, scroll down to "Bulletin Boards" at the end of the page.

The Economist

http://www.economist.com/index.html/

British magazine for discussion of a broad range of international topics.

part

2

Forbes Magazine

http://www.forbes.com/

Economic news from a business perspective from the Ditigal Tool "capitalist tool."

Foreign Affairs

http://foreignaffairs.org/

Prestigious journal for international policy.

George

http://www.georgemag.com/

Quarterly journal of politics and trends. Check out its interactive features. It is available only on America Online.

HotWired

`http://www.hotwired.com/`

This online verson of Wired Magazine proclaims its role as "defining the Web."

Intellectual Capital.com

`http://www.intellectualcapital.com/`

This online publication features weekly topics on a range of social issues that would be very effective for persuasive speeches.

National Geographic

`http://www.nationalgeographic.com/`

Includes excellent multimedia tours featuring graphics and RealAudio sound.

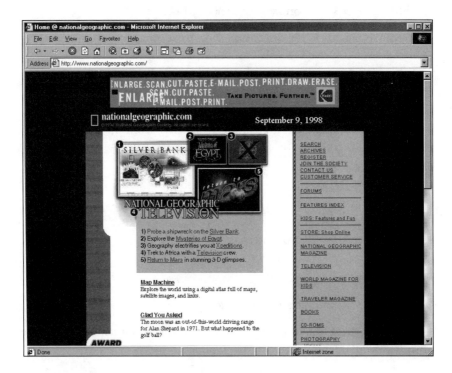

The Nation

http://www.thenation.com/

Digital version of a traditional political magazine. A special feature is its link to RadioNation, a weekly broadcast in RealAudio format originating from the Pacifica network.

National Review

http://www.nationalreview.com/

Conservative journal on political issues, published by William F. Buckley.

The New Republic

http://www.enews.com/magazines/tnr/

Journal of opinion emphasizing current political topics, offering a range of ideological perspectives from liberal to neo-conservative. The online version provides a sample of the articles in the full hard-copy edition.

part 2

Policy Review

http://www.heritage.org/heritage/p_review/
welcome.html

News and political magazine from the conservative point of view of the Heritage Foundation.

Scientific American

http://www.sciam.com/index.html/

This is the home page for *Scientific American*.

Salon Magazine

http://www.salonmagazine.com/

Find materials on popular culture and social trends in this magazine.

Slate

`http://www.slate.com/`

Online news magazine created by Microsoft, solely as an Internet political and social policy magazine. Access to this e-zine is by subscription only. However, you can try a free trial subscription.

Time

`http://www.pathfinder.com/time/`

Use the pathfinder to search for current and past issues of Time Magazine.

US News and World Report

`http://www.usnews.com/`

Weekly news journal.

Broadcast News Networks

ABC

`http://www.abcnews.com/`

The page from ABC offers links to the various national news programs on the network.

CNBC—The Leader in Business News

`http://www.cnbc.com/`

This is the home page for CNBC, the leader in business news. This site offers a business center, media clips, and a schedule of daytime and primetime guests. The user can also link to CNBC Europe and CNBC Asia from this site.

part

2

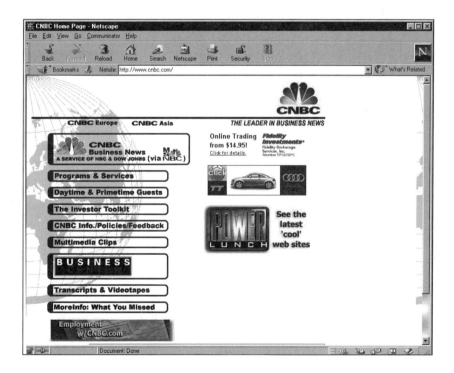

CNN Interactive

`http://cnn.com/`

Be sure to scroll down to browse the range of topics and discussion areas availble from CNN.

FOX NEWS

`http://foxnews.com/`

From the FOX you can read headlines and link to some of its news programs.

C-SPAN—Your Online Resource for Public Affairs

`http://www.c-span.org/`

C-SPAN's home page provides the user with audio and video footage, a schedule of today's happenings in Congress, a search engine, C-SPAN in the classroom, and allows the user to shop for videos and other products.

PBS

`http://www.pbs.org/`

The Public Broadcasting System is online. Many PBS programs provide a wealth of online information in conjunction notes about the programs themselves.

Legislative

The Federal News Service:

`http://www.fnsg.com/`

This is a source used by journalists to find transcripts of Congressional hearings and to find statements made by national and international leaders. It is a commercial site, and thus some of its features are for subscribers only. But the free parts are worthwhile.

U.S. House of Representatives

http://www.house.gov/

House homepage provides links to information about the legislative process, bills under deliberation and a directory for House members. The page also provides links to other government sources.

U.S. Senate

http://www.senate.gov/

Find the address for your senator. There is also a useful guide to Senate committees.

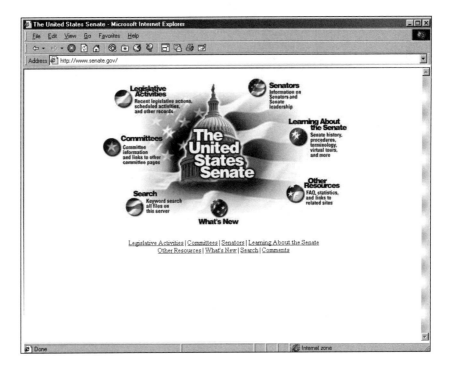

House of Representatives Internet Law Library

http://law.house.gov/

Briefing materials on a host of subjects that lawmakers deliberate. Note especially the link to http://thomas.loc.gov/bss/d105/hot-subj.html for "Law on all subjects," which provides an alphabetic topical listing of current issues. Court cases and legal briefs on a variety of issues are also included.

CWA Political/Legislative Web

http://www.cwa-legis-pol.org/

"The Communications Workers of America Web site provides the user with hot issues about federal agencies, specific state issues, a link to CWA political/legislative department, CWA Bill of Rights, and the option to write to your congressperson."

Library of Congress

http://lcweb.loc.gov/homepage/lchp.html

Library of Congress offers information in history, an exhibitions gallery, current events, legislative information, details on catalogs, collections and research references and a special bicentennial birthday page.

Policy.com

http://policy.com/

This nonpartisan site provides news and analysis of political topics.

Statistical Abstracts from the U.S. Census Bureau:

http://www.census.gov/stat_abstract/

Information you can search from the last census.

Federal Bureau of Investigation

http://www.fbi.gov/

The FBI's home page includes: community outreach programs, FBI academy information, FAQs, contacting different offices, history of the FBI, 90th anniversary ceremony, and tour information. Also included is a kid's page.

The White House

http://www.whitehouse.gov/

Send email to the president or vice president. You can also tap into various units of the Executive branch. Search the archives for past presidential statements and RealAudio files of presidential speeches.

Judicial

American Communication Association

http://www.americancomm.org/~aca/american.htm/

The ACA Center for Communication Law provides a variety of links to aspects of communication law and free speech issues.

Court TV Law Center

http://www.courttv.com/

Links from this page direct you to resources for some of the most popular cases that have been aired on this cable TV program from its case files. There are less notorious cases as well. Of special use for giving a persuasive speech are the sections on elder law and family law. Click on each to find a list of topics and brief background about some issues. To browse for topics, go to http://www.courttv.com/lawlinks/ for an alphabetic listing of cases in its lawlinks.

part

2

CyberSpace Law Center

http://www.cybersquirrel.com/clc/clcindex.html

This is an excellent source if you are looking for a topic dealing with legal issues surrounding the Internet.

Federal Courts Finder

http://www.law.emory.edu/FEDCTS/

Use this to locate decisions from circuit courts around the country.

Federal Court Locator

`http://www.law.vill.edu/Fed-Ct/fedcourt.html`

Go to Center for Information Law and Policy at Villanova University to search for decisions at various levels.

Justice Information Center

`http://www.ncjrs.org/homepage.htm/`

From its image map you can find a host of topics in law enforcement and criminal justice. Some of the downloadable documents require that you use Adobe Acrobat.

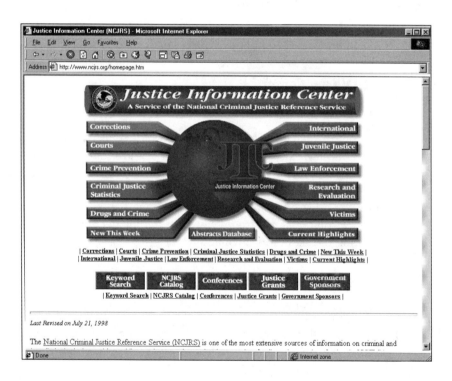

National Institute of Justice

`http://ncjrs.org/nijhome.htm/`

This is an agency of the Department of Justice that does research and makes recommendations on policies for dealing with crime problems.

Uniform Crime Reports

http://www.lib.virginia.edu/socsci/crime/

Use the University of Virginia Social Sciences Library to look up statistics on types of crime. The UVA Library uses FBI crime statistics. You can sort by types of crime and a geographic reporting unit. Follow the directions for making your selections and the form of the output of the data.

United States Department of Justice

http://www.usdoj.gov/

This cabinet agency of the federal government bills itself as the "largest law firm in the Nation."

WWW Virtual Law Library

http://www.law.indiana.edu/law/v-lib/lawindex.html

Go to the Indiana University

Legal Dictionaries

Court TV Glossary of Legal Terms

http://www.courttv.com/legalterms/glossary.html/

Alphabetic listings of legal terms.

The Law Office Dictionary

http://www.thelawoffice.com/Research/Law_Dict.htm

This is an online version of a legal dictionary from the Microsoft Network.

Legislative Indexing Vocabulary

http://lcweb.loc.gov/lexico/liv/brsearch.html

LIV terms used to label legislation at the Library of Congress. Legislative Indexing. Vocabulary terms are used in laws. When you type in a popular term, the LIV equivalent will be provided.

part

2

WWWLIA Legal Dictionary

http://www.islandnet.com/~wwlia/diction.htm/

You can find terms from American law, or for other English speaking countries with a legal system based in Anglo Saxon Common Law.

 ## Sources for Audience Analysis

Demographic Studies:

Bureau of Labor Statistics

http://stats.bls.gov//

Use this source to find socioeconomic data.

Center for Demography and Ecology

http://www.ssc.wisc.edu/cde/

The University of Wisconsin at Madison's Center for Demography and Ecology includes information on demography from training seminar schedules to online publications.

Social Science Research Computing Center's Page of Other Demography Research Centers

http://www.spc.uchicago.edu/wwwusr/orgs/coa/coa_cent.html

The SSRC at the University of Chicago has collected links dealing with demography, including sponsored population research centers, sponsored exploratory centers on aging, other demography research centers and related government agencies.

United Nation's Information on Population and Demography

http://www.library.yale.edu/un/un3b8.htm

This site provides texts, charts, and facts from the U.N. on population and demography. It also provide links to other demography sites.

World Wide Web Virtual Library Demography and Population Studies

`http://coombs.anu.edu.au/ResFacilities/Demography`
`Page.html/`

This is a mammoth list of links to places around the globe on various facets of demography. It is maintained by the Australian National University.

University of Virginia Social Sciences Data Center County and City Data

`http://www.lib.virginia.edu/socsci/ccdb/`

This is a handy interactive page for finding demographic data for many cities in the country. The County and City Books are based principally on U.S. Census data.

U.S. Census Bureau

`http://www.census.gov/`

Find reports from the last census as well as frequent updates on the U.S. population and economic indicators. The page offers a variety of tools for accessing demographic data. A particularly useful tool for learning census information about a particular community is found at the U.S. Gazetteer link. Go to http://www.census.gov/cgi-bin/gazetteer/. You can use this page to search for demographic data by zip code.

Psychographics:

PopNet

`http://www.popnet.org/`

This is a population information resource. This site offers a comprehensive directory of population related Web sites, available by keyword search, topic, organization, or by using the interactive map.

part
2

United Nations Population Information Network (POPIN)

`http://www.undp.org/popin/`

This site offers information on the trends of world population and regional population.

Internet Domain Survey

`http://www.nw.com/zone/WWW/top.html`

This is a demographic page for the World Wide Web. Statistics, including number of hosts, on the Web are available as well as past survey results and related links.

Public Opinion Studies:

The Gallup Organization

`http://www.gallup.com/`

This is the home page for Gallup. On it you will find links to a few of its most recent studies on national opinions. Harris Polls: (See Institute for Research in Social Science Public below).

The General Social Survey

`http://www.icpsr.umich.edu/gss/about/gss/gssintro.htm/`

Use the omnibus personal interview of U.S. households done by the National Opinion Research Center to find attitudes on a variety of social issues. The Subject Index provides an alphabetic listing by topics. Use the GSS Module Index to see batteries of questions on themes.

GVU Center's WWW User Surveys

`http://www.cc.gatech.edu/gvu/user_surveys/`

This site provides 10 survey reports from 10,000 Internet users. Questions in the survey came from topics such as general demographics, Internet shopping, Internet banking, technology demographics, Internet usage, and others.

The National Election Studies Guide to Public Opinion and Electoral Behavior

http://www.umich.edu/~nes/nesguide/gd-index.htm#1/

The National Election Studies (NES) is affiliated with the University of Michigan Institute for Social Research. This page provides data about religious affiliation, ideological identification, and results of opinion research on a wide range of social and political topics.

LA Times Polls Index

http://www.latimes.com/HOME/NEWS/POLLS/

Most of the polls are on California issues.

Yankelovich

http://www.yankelovich.com/

Use this site to learn about studies conducted by Yankelovich. There are descriptions of a few studies, but to access the entirety of each report, you need to purchase Yankelovich reports.

Multimedia

Adobe Systems

http://www.adobe.com/

Adobe's Photoshop is the standard in the field. Another useful product is Adobe's PDF, (Portable Document Format) for converting a variety of types of multimedia file formats for use on HTML pages.

Astound, Inc.

http://www.astoundinc.com/

Astound is one of the most useful software packages for creating presentations for public speaking. From this page, you can download free trial versions of Astound or StudioM. If you use Astound or Studio M, Astound, Inc. also offers a free encoder that converts your presentation to a web document and the Astound WebMotion program that works with JAVA equipped browsers.

Beginners Guide to HTML

http://www.ncsa.uiuc.edu/General/Internet/WWW/
HTMLPrimer.html/

This is a primer for getting started using HTML.

The Bare Bones Guide to HTML

http://werbach.com/barebones/

This is an online guide to coding HTML specifications. It also explains Netscape extensions.

HTML at InSysTech Interactive Multimedia

part
2

http://www.insystechim.com/HTMLlinks.htm

InSysTech Interactive Multimedia's page on multimedia on the Web offers the user links to many audio, video, and animation sites. It also provides news and online demos.

Corel Home Page

http://www.corel.ca/

Check out this page for information about Corel products. Of special value to public speakers is Corel Presentations for creating multimedia slide shows.

DSP

http://www.dspg.com/

Put sound files on your Web page compressed with True Speech. The DSP page offers a free download of the software you need.

HTML Goodies

http://www.htmlgoodies.com/

This compendium of resources for developing Web pages was created by Dr. Joe Burns. You can find free art work and scripts for your Web page.

Microsoft Downloads

`http://www.microsoft.com/msdownload/`

For users of Windows, this is a great source for downloading free software. A number of multimedia tools used for Web viewing are available, including the Microsoft Internet Explorer, the PowerPoint Animation viewer, the PowerPoint Viewer, ActiveX Controls, Microsoft's VRML Viewer, and Web authoring tools that work with the various components of the Microsoft Office. This page also links you to product information about PowerPoint, the component of the Microsoft Office most useful to public speakers for creating presentations.

JASC

`http://www.jasc.com/`

JASC is the producer of Paint Shop Pro, one of the most versatile graphics programs for manipulating bitmap images.

Netscape

`http://home.netscape.com/`

part
2

Download the latest version of Netscape, one of the premier Web page browsers. The Netcenter provides additional links to resources for using the Internet and creating Web pages.

Marke Pesce—Outside the Light-Cone

`http://hyperreal.com/~mpesce/`

Pesce is a pioneer in developing virtual reality. This is his Web page with links to the various papers that he has presented.

RealNetworks—The Home of RealAudio:

`http://www.realaudio.com/`

Go here to download a copy of the RealPlayer for receiving streamed audio and video in RealAudio and RealVideo formats.

Webmonkey Tutorials

http://www.hotwired.com/webmonkey/teachingtool/
index.html/

This page features tips from the creators of *HotWired*.

Live Chat

Propaganda Public Forum

http://carmen.artsci.washington.edu/propaganda/
intermediate.html/

This bulletin board features discussion of persuasion and propaganda
on the Net. Its main page, http://carmen.artsci.washington.edu/
propaganda/contents.htm, features tutorials on propaganda techniques.

WebChat Broadcasting System

`http://www.wbs.net/webchat3.so?i=1/`

This online forum hosts a number of hubs for ongoing conversation. For public speaking topics, the Current Events hub includes political and social topics.

Yahoo! Events

`http://events.yahoo.com/`

Find a list of chat activities in a wide range of subjects and in many venues.

 ## Live Events

Broadcast.com

`http://www.broadcast.com/`

This page provides a daily update of scheduled live events you can tune into using RealAudio.

C-SPAN Online (RealAudio)

`http://www.broadcast.com/television/c-span/`

Listen to sessions of the House and Senate and find a directory of what is going on on the Hill.

Dick Becker's Internet LIVE—News Stations

`http://www.geocities.com/ResearchTriangle/1803/`
`news.htm`

At this site, the user can listen to radio stations (via RealAudio) from all over the world broadcasting live.

FedNet

`http://www.fednet.net/`

You can listen to RealAudio coverage of select House and Senate committee hearings as well as floor action from Congress at this site. FedNet also maintains past RealAudio files.

NetGuide

`http://www.netguide.com/`

Find out when live events and chats take place. Subjects include stories in the news, shopping, health, the Internet, money, travel, entertainment, life, and sports.

U.S. Department of Defense Live News Briefings

`http://www.defenselink.mil/briefings/`

This site provides live news briefings pertaining to Department of Defense. There are also text archives of past months' and years' briefings.

Sites and Sounds from ABC

`http://www.realaudio.com/contentp/abc.html`

This page offers news reports and commentary on the day's news.

The YO! Radio Project

`http://www.pacificnews.org/yo/radio/`

From Youth Outlook in the San Francisco Bay area, this page provides weekly commentaries on problems faced by young people. The commentaries are presented in RealAudio.

Historical Archives

American Memory Collection

`http://lcweb2.loc.gov/`

Search or browse for historical documents in the Library of Congress.

Biography.com

`http://www.biography.com/`

Search this database of famous people to learn how every life has a story.

Douglass

`http://douglass.speech.nwu.edu/`

Use this archive to read texts of famous American orators. The files are organized by speaker, speech title, chronology and by subject. There are also notes on rhetorical studies for courses at Northwestern University, where the site resides.

Gateway to Presidential Libraries

`http://www.nara.gov/nara/president/address.html`

The National Archive maintains this page as a directory to holdings at the libraries for each of the U.S. presidents since Hoover.

NARA Archival Information Locator (NAIL)

`http://www.nara.gov/nara/nail.html`

NAIL is a searchable database that contains information about a wide variety of holdings at the National Archives & Records Administration. Users can search and retrieve digital copies of selected textual documents, photographs, maps and more.

part

2

History Channel

`http://www.historychannel.com/`

Equipped with a "This Day in History" feature, this site offers the user many options. The user can search, take a history quiz, vote in a poll, and browse general history news.

Inaugural Addresses of U.S. Presidents

`http://www.columbia.edu/acis/bartleby/inaugural/`

This collection from Columbia University links you to each of the Presidential Inauguration Addresses from George Washington to George Bush. For both Clinton Inaugural Addresses, you can go to the White House, http://www.whitehouse.gov.

MSU Vincent Voice Library

http://web.msu.edu/vincent/

From this archive you can download .au and .wav files, including some recordings of U.S. Presidents and other historical figures or events.

White House Audio Archive

http://library.whitehouse.gov/?request=audio/

Go to this page to listen to Saturday Radio Addresses presented by President Clinton. The page includes a search engine that you can use to find a speech by topic area or date.

Supreme Court Oral Argument: The Oral Argument Page

http://oyez.nwu.edu/

You can listen to actual voice recordings of oral argument in cases heard by the U.S. Supreme Court. This site requires RealAudio.

African American History

http://www.msstate.edu/Archives/History/USA/
Afro-Amer/afro.html

This site offers many links and archived documents on African-American history. The links are categorized into: slavery, people, military, states and regions, and texts.

WebCorp Historical Speeches Archive

http://www.webcorp.com/sounds/

Sound bites from speeches since the 1930s on a variety of topics. There is also a video collection from the Nixon era and the Watergate scandal. Some sound offerings are available in RealAudio.

News Archives

Back in Time

http://allpolitics.com/1997/gen/news/back.time/

This is a collection of selected articles from issues of *Time Magazine* dating to the 1920s.

CNN Interactive Video Vault

`http://www.cnn.com/video_vault/index.html/`

Apple QuickTime movies and video clips using the VIVO format are featured. You can find highlights from the latest stories carried on CNN as well as clips from stories from the past three years.

Vanderbilt Television News Archive

`http://tvnews.vanderbilt.edu/`

Find text transcripts of TV news programs on the major networks since 1968.

Documentation

part

2

Your Citation for Exemplary Research

There's another detail left for us to handle—the formal citing of electronic sources in academic papers. The very factor that makes research on the Internet exciting is the same factor that makes referencing these sources challenging: their dynamic nature. A journal article exists, either in print or on microfilm, virtually forever. A document on the Internet can come, go, and change without warning. Because the purpose of citing sources is to allow another scholar to retrace your argument, a good citation allows a reader to obtain information from your primary sources, to the extent possible. This means you need to include not only information on when a source was posted on the Internet (if available) but also when you obtained the information.

The two arbiters of form for academic and scholarly writing are the Modern Language Association (MLA) and the American Psychological Association (APA); both organizations have established styles for citing electronic publications.

MLA Style

In the second edition of the *MLA Style Manual,* the MLA recommends the following formats:

- URLs: URLs are enclosed in angle brackets (<>) and contain the access mode identifier, the formal name for such indicators as "http" or "ftp." If a URL must be split across two lines, break it only after a slash (/). Never introduce a hyphen at the end of the first line. The URL should include all the parts necessary to identify uniquely the file/document being cited.

  `<http://www.csun.edu/~rtvfdept/home/index.html>`

- A complete online reference contains the title of the project or database (underlined); the name of the editor of the project or database (if given); electronic publication information, including version number (if relevant and if not part of the title); date of electronic publication or latest update; name of any sponsoring institution or organization; date of access; and electronic address.

- If you cannot find some of the information, then include the information that is available.

The MLA also recommends that you print or download electronic documents, freezing them in time for future reference.

World Wide Web Site   The elements of a proper citation are the name of the person creating the site (reversed), followed by a period, the title of the site (underlined), or, if there is no title, a description such as home page (such a description is neither placed in quotes nor underlined). Then specify the name of any school, organization, or other institution affiliated with the site and follow it with your date of access and the URL of the page.

```
Gotthoffer, Doug. RTVF Dept. Website. California
     State University, Northridge. 1 September 1998.
```

Some electronic references are truly unique to the online domain. These include email, newsgroup postings, MUDs (multiuser domains) or MOOs (multiuser domains, object oriented), and IRCs (Internet Relay Chats).

Email   In citing email messages, begin with the writer's name (reversed) followed by a period, then the title of the message (if any) in quotations as it appears in the subject line. Next comes a description of the message, typically "Email to," and the recipient (e.g., "the author"), and finally the date of the message.

Davis, Jeffrey. "Web Writing Resources." Email to
    Nora Davis. 5 July 1998.

Sommers, Laurice. "Re: College Admissions Practices."
    Email to the author. 12 August 1998.

List Servers and Newsgroups   In citing these references, begin with the author's name (reversed) followed by a period. Next include the title of the document (in quotes) from the subject line, followed by the words "Online posting" (not in quotes). Follow this with the date of posting. For list servers, include the date of access, the name of the list (if known), and the online address of the list's moderator or administrator. For newsgroups, follow "Online posting" with the date of posting, the date of access, and the name of the newsgroup, prefixed with news: and enclosed in angle brackets.

part
2

Applebaum, Dale. "Educational Variables." Online
    posting. 29 Jan. 1998. Higher Education
    Discussion Group. 30 January 1993
    <jlucidoj@unc.edu>.

Gostl, Jack. "Re: Mr. Levitan." Online posting.
    13 June 1997. 20 June 1997
    <news:alt.edu.bronxscience>.

MUDs, MOOs, and IRCs   Citations for these online sources take the form of the name of the speaker(s) followed by a period. Then comes the description and date of the event, the name of the forum, the date of access, and the online address prefixed by "telnet://".

Guest. Personal interview. 13 August 1998
    <telnet//du.edu 8888>.

APA Style

The *Publication Manual of the American Psychological Association* (4th ed.) is fairly dated in its handling of online sources, having been published before the rise of the WWW and the generally recognized format for URLs. The format that follows is based on the APA manual, with modifications proposed by Russ Dewey <www.psychwww.com/ resource/apacrib.htm>. It's important to remember that, unlike the MLA, the APA does not include temporary or transient sources (e.g., letters, phone calls, etc.) in its "References" page, preferring to handle them in in-text citations exclusively. This rule holds for electronic sources as well: email, MOOs/MUDs, list server postings, etc., are not included in the "References" page, merely cited in text, for example, "But Wilson has rescinded his earlier support for these policies" (Charles Wilson, personal email to the author, 20 November 1996). But also note that many list server and Usenet groups and MOOs actually archive their correspondences, so that there is a permanent site (usually a Gopher or FTP server) where those documents reside. In that case, you would want to find the archive and cite it as an unchanging source. Strictly speaking, according to the APA manual, a file from an FTP site should be referenced as follows:

```
Deutsch, P. (1991). "Archie-An electronic directory
    service for the Internet" [Online]. Available
    FTP: ftp.sura.net Directory: pub/archie/docs
    File: whatis.archie.
```

However, the increasing familiarity of Net users with the convention of a URL makes the prose description of how to find a file <"Available FTP: ftp.sura.net Directory: pub/archie/docs File: whatis.archie"> unnecessary. Simply specifying the URL should be enough.

So, with such a modification of the APA format, citations from the standard Internet sources would appear as follows.

FTP (File Transfer Protocol) Sites To cite files available for downloading via FTP, give the author's name (if known), the publication date (if available and if different from the date accessed), the full title of the paper (capitalizing only the first word and proper nouns), the address of the FTP site along with the full path necessary to access the file, and the date of access.

part

2

Deutsch, P. (1991) "Archie-An electronic directory
service for the Internet." [Online]. Available:
ftp://ftp.sura.net/pub/archie/docs/whatis.archie.

WWW Sites (World Wide Web) To cite files available for viewing or
downloading via the World Wide Web, give the author's name (if
known), the year of publication (if known and if different from the date
accessed), the full title of the article, and the title of the complete work
(if applicable) in italics. Include any additional information (such as versions, editions, or revisions) in parentheses immediately following the
title. Include the full URL (the http address) and the date of visit.

Burka, L. P. (1993). A hypertext history of multiuser dungeons. MUDdex. http://www.utopia.com/
talent/lpb/muddex/essay/ (13 Jan. 1997).

Tilton, J. (1995). Composing good HTML (Vers. 2.0.6).
http://www.cs.cmu.edu/~tilt/cgh/ (1 Dec. 1996).

part 2

Telnet Sites List the author's name or alias (if known), the date of
publication (if available and if different from the date accessed), the title
of the article, the title of the full work (if applicable) or the name of the
Telnet site in italics, and the complete Telnet address, followed by a
comma and directions to access the publication (if applicable). Last, give
the date of visit in parentheses.

Dava (#472). (1995, 3 November). A deadline.
*General (#554). Internet Public Library.
telnet://ipl.sils.umich.edu:8888, @peek 25 on
#554 (9 Aug. 1996).

Help. Internet public library.
telnet://ipl.org:8888/, help (1 Dec. 1996).

Synchronous Communications (MOOs, MUDs, IRC, etc.) Give the name of
the speaker(s), the complete date of the conversation being referenced in
parentheses (if different from the date accessed), and the title of the ses-
sion (if applicable). Next, list the title of the site in italics, the protocol
and address (if applicable), and any directions necessary to access the
work. If there is additional information such as archive addresses or
file numbers (if applicable), list the word "Available," a colon, and
the archival information. Last, list the date of access, enclosed in

parentheses. Personal interviews do not need to be listed in the References, but do need to be included in parenthetic references in the text (see the APA *Publication Manual*).

```
Basic IRC commands. irc undernet.org, /help (13 Jan.
    1996).
```

```
Cross, J. (1996, February 27). Netoric's Tuesday
    cafe: Why use MUDs in the writing classroom?
    MediaMoo. telenet://purple-crayon.media.mit.edu:
    8888, @go Tuesday. Available: ftp://daedalus.com/
    pub/ACW/NETORIC/catalog.96a (tc 022796.log).
    (1 Mar. 1996).
```

Gopher Sites List the author's name (if applicable), the year of publication (if known and if different from the date accessed), the title of the file or paper, and the title of the complete work (if applicable). Include any print publication information (if available) followed by the protocol (i.e., gopher://) and the path necessary to access the file. List the date that the file was accessed in parentheses immediately following the path.

```
Massachusetts Higher Education Coordinating
    Council. (1994) [Online]. Using coordination
    and collaboration to address change. Available:
    gopher://gopher.mass.edu:170/00gopher_root%3A%5B_
    hecc%5D_plan.
```

Email, Listservs, and Newsgroups Give the author's name (if known), the date of the correspondence in parentheses (if known and if different from the date accessed), the subject line from the posting, and the name of the list (if known) in italics. Next, list the address of the listserv or newsgroup. Include any archival information after the address, listing the word "Available" and a colon and the protocol and address of the archive. Last, give the date accessed enclosed in parentheses. Do not include personal email in the list of References. See the APA *Publication Manual* for information on in-text citations.

```
Bruckman, A. S. MOOSE crossing proposal.
    mediamoo@media.mit.edu (20 Dec. 1994).
```

```
Heilke, J. (1996, May 3). Re: Webfolios. acw-l@ttacs.
ttu.edu. Available: http://www.ttu.edu/lists/acw-l/
    9605 (31 Dec. 1996).
```

part **2**

```
Laws, R. UMI thesis publication. alt.education.
    distance (3 Jan. 1996).
```

Other authors and educators have proposed similar extensions to the APA style, too. You can find URLs to these pages at

```
www.psychwww.com/resource/apacrib.htm
```

and

```
www.nouveaux.com/guides.htm
```

Another frequently-referenced set of extensions is available at

```
www.uvm.edu/~ncrane/estyles/apa.htm
```

Remember, "frequently-referenced" does not equate to "correct" or even "desirable." Check with your professor to see if your course or school has a preference for an extended APA style.

part

2

Glossary

Your Own Private Glossary

The Glossary in this book contains reference terms you'll find useful as you get started on the Internet. After a while, however, you'll find yourself running across abbreviations, acronyms, and buzzwords whose definitions will make more sense to you once you're no longer a novice (or "newbie"). That's the time to build a glossary of your own. For now, the 2DNet Webopædia gives you a place to start.

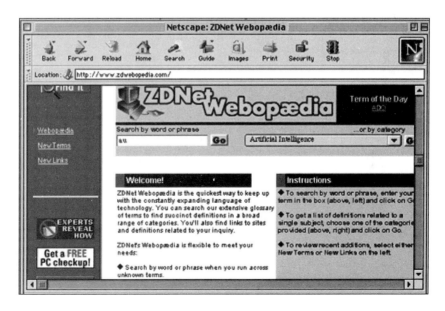

alias
A simple email address that can be used in place of a more complex one.

AVI
Audio Video Interleave. A video compression standard developed for use with Microsoft Windows. Video clips on the World Wide Web are usually available in both AVI and QuickTime formats.

bandwidth
Internet parlance for capacity to carry or transfer information such as email and Web pages.

BBS
Bulletin Board System. A dial-up computer service that allows users to post messages and download files. Some BBSs are connected to and provide access to the Internet, but many are self-contained.

browser
The computer program that lets you view the contents of Web sites.

client
A program that runs on your personal computer and supplies you with Internet services, such as getting your mail.

cyberspace
The whole universe of information that is available from computer networks. The term was coined by science fiction writer William Gibson in his novel *Neuromancer,* published in 1984.

DNS
See **domain name server.**

domain
A group of computers administered as a single unit, typically belonging to a single organization such as a university or corporation.

domain name
A name that identifies one or more computers belonging to a single domain. For example, "apple.com".

domain name server
A computer that converts domain names into the numeric addresses used on the Internet.

download

Copying a file from another computer to your computer over the Internet.

email

Electronic mail.

emoticon

A guide to the writer's feelings, represented by typed characters, such as the Smiley :-). Helps readers understand the emotions underlying a written message.

FAQ

Frequently Asked Questions

flame

A rude or derogatory message directed as a personal attack against an individual or group.

flame war

An exchange of flames (see above).

FTP

File Transfer Protocol, a method of moving files from one computer to another over the Internet.

home page

A page on the World Wide Web that acts as a starting point for information about a person or organization.

hypertext

Text that contains embedded *links* to other pages of text. Hypertext enables the reader to navigate between pages of related information by following links in the text.

LAN:

Local Area Network. A computer network that is located in a concentrated area, such as offices within a building.

link

A reference to a location on the Web that is embedded in the text of the Web page. Links are usually highlighted with a different color or underline to make them easily visible.

list server
Strictly speaking, a computer program that administers electronic mailing lists, but also used to denote such lists or discussion groups, as in "the writer's list server."

lurker
A passive reader of an Internet *newsgroup*. A lurker reads messages, but does not participate in the discussion by posting or responding to messages.

mailing list
A subject-specific automated e-mail system. Users subscribe and receive e-mail from other users about the subject of the list.

modem
A device for connecting two computers over a telephone line.

newbie
A new user of the Internet.

newsgroup
A discussion forum in which all participants can read all messages and public replies between the participants.

pages
All the text, graphics, pictures, and so forth, denoted by a single URL beginning with the identifier "http://".

plug-in
A third-party software program that will lend a web browser (Netscape, Internet Explorer, etc.) additional features.

quoted
Text in an email message or newsgroup posting that has been set off by the use of vertical bars or > characters in the left-hand margin.

search engine
A computer program that will locate Web sites or files based on specified criteria.

secure
A Web page whose contents are encrypted when sending or receiving information.

server
A computer program that moves information on request, such as a Web server that sends pages to your browser.

Smiley
See **emoticon.**

snail mail
Mail sent the old fashioned way: Write a letter, put it in an envelope, stick on a stamp, and drop it in the mailbox.

spam
Spam is to the Internet as unsolicited junk mail is to the postal system.

URL
Uniform Resource Locator: The notation for specifying addresses on the World Wide Web (e.g. http://www.abacon.com or ftp://ftp.abacon.com).

Usenet
The section of the Internet devoted to *newsgroups.*

Web browser
A program used to navigate and access information on the World Wide Web. Web browsers convert html coding into a display of pictures, sound, and words.

Web site
A collection of World Wide Web pages, usually consisting of a home page and several other linked pages.